Curriculum Architecture:

Creating a Place of Our Own

Curriculum Architecture
Creating a Place of Our Own

Mary Louise Hawkins
M. Dolores Graham

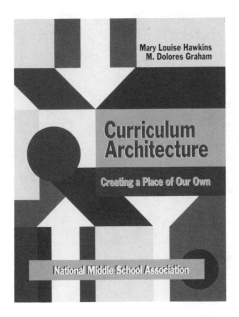

NATIONAL MIDDLE SCHOOL ASSOCIATION

National Middle School Association
2600 Corporate Exchange Drive, Suite 370
Columbus, Ohio 43231-1672

Mary Louise Hawkins' long career started in journalism but soon shifted to education with teaching positions in Oklahoma, California, and Missouri. Curriculum development, grant writing, and pioneering in change have been focuses of Dr. Hawkins' efforts in recent years.

M. Dolores Graham is the Principal of Cross Keys Middle School in Florissant, Missouri, the second school she has led to national recognition as a school of excellence. A former English teacher, Dr. Graham's commitment to kids has undergirded her willingness to tackle the tough job of making substantive changes.

The National Middle School Association is grateful to these two close friends and professional leaders for preparing this timely volume. Its appearance coincides nicely with the national curriculum reform effort. Appreciation is also extended to Mary Mitchell for her painstaking work in preparing the manuscript for printing.

ISBN: 1-56090-081-4

Contents

Schools are filled with unhappy people. Our children are crying—from discord, from chaos, from pain, from loneliness. Our teachers are crying—from loss of effectiveness, loss of equilibrium, loss of stature—trapped in a profession whose demands have changed. A dissonance of sounds, a clash of score reverberates as these two anguished human spirits collide in a setting called "school."

We are silent…They bring discord

We are orderly…They bring hunger

We are directive…They bring restlessness

We are of single mind…They bring differences

We are content bound…They bring fragility

We want to orchestrate changes that will put the school's world in synch with the children. We don't wish to jerk them into our world as schools now do, but we wish to be adults who enter their world, able to reflect upon our actions and adjust as the children play out their role in school.

Foreword

A refreshing, remarkable, and revealing treatise on the current "hot topic" of curriculum reform awaits readers of *Curriculum Architecture*. With style, boldness, and a hard-to-deny sense of reality, this book provides an important, but often overlooked perspective on the business of designing a curriculum for young adolescents. Its central message surfaces frequently and with clarity—each school must create its own curriculum based on its own study of its students, its community, its faculty, and with the real involvement of the students themselves. The task is to design "a place of our own." The authors, a pair of paradigm pioneers, speak from experience, for they have chosen to lead in charting a new route, one filled with tensions and roadblocks, but ultimate satisfaction.

A wonderfully engaging review of our society and its recent changes—which will bring a smile of remembrance to those of us over forty—opens this publication. Before readers have gone through its eight chapters they will be amused, occasionally angered, often enlightened, and finally well-armed with advice and guidelines for building a curriculum that is learner and learning-centered.

Examples and illustrations are plentiful. The message of this monograph is timely, wise, and challenging—though those not really serious about reconceptualizing the middle level curriculum and those not able to make the paradigm shift needed will want to shrug it off. Those of us active in middle level education, however, need all the help we can muster as we seek to reform the middle school curriculum —and this volume offers both an important point of view and guidance in taking the big step beyond organizational change to the necessary alteration of the school's culture, its values, and its collective beliefs. This publication has as well what may be an unrecognized but ultimately a special importance. Its philosophical foundation is in line with a growing recognition that the problem of alienation and the resulting violence is not going to be solved by more cops and more prisons, but rather by providing educational experiences during the foundational years that touch students' consciousness, their character, and give them hope.

—John H. Lounsbury
Publications Editor,
NMSA

Preface

This monograph was born out of a combination of frustration and commitment. Two full and lusty careers spent in public education should be crowned by accolades and an internal sense of well-being that comes from knowing the job was well done. Yet, we two find ourselves at this career apex with a hollow spot in our very centers. There is a sense of incompleteness; our professional commitment has not been adequately expressed.

Artisans, those good at their craft, can see themselves at work, using all they know how to do. They can gaze at their product with satisfaction. But we, in education, labor in a softer science, a more abstract art. We find that we have been unable to do all we know how to do, unable to fully actualize what the yield of experience and knowledge tells us to do.

Rather than go away sad, or feel diminished in some way, we attempted with this monograph to reach out to others so that the baton may be passed more easily to the next generation of leaders.

Curriculum Architecture tells what we have come to believe and to know about the matter of designing curriculum. Its sum underscores the concept that curriculum is not a naturally occurring substance like an element from a Periodic Chart. It is man-made. Like many things man creates, curriculum has a framework that outlines its very nature. Many professionals use frameworks. An architect's plans provide a framework for a building; a computer engineer's designs create a framework for a new product line; a football coach's diagrams of plays use a framework of X's and O's to defeat crafty opponents. All of these frameworks, or designs, define the very nature of what is to be

> There is a sense of incompleteness; our professional commitment has not been adequately expressed

created. They may be called *architectures*. Our hope is that all involved in the education of our children will recognize that curriculum architecture is to be debated, is to be changed, is to be created, is to take form from the human mind. As Willy Loman in *Death of a Salesman* says, "Attention must be paid." Curriculum deserves attention.

We do not see ourselves as disillusioned at the end of a career passed over by the acceleration of events like Willy Loman. Instead, we see that our time could run out before we finish.

Curricular change must accelerate. Youngsters are at stake. And, we intend to be around to see it happen. May this summation that describes curriculum in terms of an architectural framework create curricular conversations that hasten that day.

Mary Louise Hawkins
M. Dolores Graham

February, 1994

Chapter One

The Change Imperative

nd so . . . Here we are . . .
The Berlin Wall has fallen. The Cold War Era has yielded to a new world order. The U.S.S.R. has been dissolved. The world is in the process of transformational change. Yet "school" persists.

The word that most characterizes the essence of today is "change." The modern world, physically seen from space so tranquilly spinning on its axis, is psychologically accelerating to a super nova speed.

It is yet to be seen how humankind will adapt to such a tumultuous environment. It is clear, however, that as a professional group, educators are among the last to recognize the impact of being in a supercharged change environment.

Common life examples of rapid change abound, yet still startle. Swatch watches already are antiques. So is Pacman. These artifacts, so lately a central part of our mainstream culture, are now featured drawing cards at flea markets held in decaying drive-in movie lots far-flung across even the most rural of America's landscape. The word "antique" itself has changed to mean something only five years old, not fifty or a hundred years old.

Students in middle schools today were not even born when the movie series *Star Wars* made its impact on America's conscience. To those who guide the lives of young adolescents, *Star Wars the Trilogy* remains the symbol for future life; to middle schoolers, it is the only life they have ever known.

And it is not only technology that fuels our change environment. Some aspects of change come from gigantic leaps and turnarounds in current thought. For years, those who tried to subdue the art of ski jumping were judged on their ability to lay their bodies almost horizontally atop their ski tips tightly pressed together to provide a streamlined dynamic for air flow. In 1990, Saturday TV sports pictured skier after skier hurtling through the air stretching for every inch of distance that fine form could yield. To the casual viewer, a jarring image appeared in 1992. The jumpers' ski tips spread in a V-shape! This change represents not a fad, not a difference in some judge's eye of what constitutes beauty in form, but a new understanding of how to wrench one more precious inch in distance through aerodynamic form.

The winter Olympics showcased half of the long jumpers in a V-shape and another half in the now old fashioned over-the-tip-of-the-skis form. Even skiers, who have such a precise yardstick of achievement as feet and inches, are personally not yet ready to fully embrace a change that virtually overnight rendered obsolete their skill, their practice, their training, their very form.

In another sports arena, a season ticket holder can label as heroic the specter of the one lone hockey player still skating without a helmet. Perhaps, this iron man is symbolic of the pride and sense of destiny reflected in the visage of the last shaman on earth.

Someday, from outer space, we may view earth spinning wildly in pace with the inner world of change. But, to date, throughout the world's acceleration, "school" has persisted. Teachers have changed what they teach very little in a hundred years. The battle lines are now drawn, however, between those who resist change and those who promote change with, not yet, a decisive tip of the balance in either direction.

Yet, suspended across this contentiousness is not a matter of a sports victory won in inches, not a matter of capitalizing on consumer yearnings, but precious children. The time for educators to embrace change is here.

TALKING POINTS TO JUSTIFY CHANGE

But, citizens query, "Why can't schools be the way they used to be?" Parents join in such discussions with, "If schools were good enough for me, they are good enough for anybody." Such strong, seemingly irrefutable positions require a logical and convincing response.

Talking point number 1.

The students in classrooms today are not like any that have been in our classrooms in this century. The portrait of the American adolescent goes beyond the fads and life-styles that have demarked the decades encompassing puberty in the past. Those past decades are easily named by a song phrase, a clothing style, or sets of behaviors reserved for youth alone: the fringed silhouette of the 20s girls—the Wildroot slicked hair, black pants and pink shirts of the 50s guys—the heavily painted micro bus of the 60s—or the neon colored rollerblades and moussed hair of the 90s.

The changes that form an imperative for schools emanate from the very center of the human being. Just as the pace of change startles, so does the portrait of the American adolescent.

One in four children lives in poverty according to the final report of the National Commission on Children. These children come to school with survival needs so great that they must supersede any agenda that school may set as a priority. Children may not have eaten. They may not be sure of where they will stay tomorrow. They may be "given away" at any time to a relative close or far. Their environment outside of school is unsafe and characterized by shootings, neighborhood conflicts, and instability. In fact, families with children are the fastest growing segment of the homeless population. Special programs, supportive environments, and special intervention techniques are needed to reach the children of poverty.

In past decades, children of poverty could find a productive place in society by their own initiative without an education. They became assembly line workers, miners, laborers, oil drillers. They formed the mass of our middle class. Immigrants and high school dropouts were still upwardly mobile. Heightening the plight of poverty is the realization that without an education children can-

> The changes that form an imperative for schools emanate from the very center of the human being.

not become productive adults, joining the middle class. The oil rigs in Oklahoma are idle, stacked up. There is no further need for miners when the bulldozers have covered the mines and capped them with man-planted forests. The assembly line workers have been replaced by robots or their jobs have been moved to a foreign country, while the day labor jobs typically filled by teens have been scornfully left for illegal immigrants, political refugees, and the 90s equivalent of the "boat people." This very fact of survival is a part of the change in the portrait of the American adolescent.

The portrait of the contemporary American adolescent is a mosaic that demands a different school, a different curriculum.

Another airbrush that lends texture to the portrait of the American adolescent is the characteristics of the presumably resilient and capable children. Even these children are from mainly single parent homes, where the head of the household is typically a single, working mother. A large number of these children exhibit high, at-risk factors and experience academic, interpersonal, and social failure at school. At-risk characteristics include: children home alone more than two hours a day, parents who did not graduate from high school, siblings who dropped out of school, limited English proficiency in the home, and children encircled by crime or substance abuse.

A change for the better in this stark portrait seems beyond reach. The children who will be the schools' future clients are coming predominantly from teenage mothers, one in ten of whom takes illegal drugs during pregnancy, and from families below the poverty line. The lack of access to health care and the lack of trust in societal institutions such as governments and schools do not make for any easier clientele to come.

The record of how schools have fared with these American adolescents is none too promising. While the American adolescent is undergoing change, the like of which schools have never seen, achievement scores did not improve, businesses and universities bemoan preparation levels of students they interview and hire, percentages of dropouts increased, and although not documented, the number of failing grades registered in math, science, and social studies piles higher. The barometers of the lack of schools' success as reflected in numerous government reports and media coverage of data about youth (Cross, 1990; *U.S Children and Their Families*, 1989) make the following statements frightening:

> Of all students retained once,
>   50% drop out of school.

> Of all students retained twice,
>   98% drop out of school.

> For every hour a child is home alone,
>   his achievement decreases proportionately.

> More than half of all children spend one hour
>   home alone.

> One of every four children spends more than
>   two hours home alone.

> Of all children, 31% say their mother is
>   rarely or never home when they arrive.

The portrait of the contemporary American adolescent is, indeed, a mosaic that demands a different school, a different curriculum.

Talking point number 2:
Schools really can't be the way they used to be because students learn differently. Twenty years ago, students learned primarily through auditory and visual sensors. Thus, adults' memories of sitting in a hard wooden chair with a strange arm appendage in front tucked behind four or five other like seats in rows while a teacher presented knowledge are accurate and was accepted. Those yesteryear students survived lessons if they could see them, read them or hear them. But for now and into the next century, learners are mainly **tactile and kinesthetic** oriented as many teachers have learned by administering learning styles in-

ventories. It is as if these two senses, previously dormant, have been activated. In the 90s, students must experience to learn; whereas in the past, those who could not succeed in school didn't stay the course.

Twenty years ago, students learned primarily by deducing meaning from facts. Students of the next century remember facts better if meaning and application comes first. As students search for meaning, they need to be tactilely and kinesthetically involved.

Twenty years ago, students were presented with linear and sequential procedures and processes. It seemed to have made sense to present history chronologically. Students willingly accepted the teacher's need to organize knowledge in some systematic way. Nouns come first, verbs come next. Whole integers come first. The Colonial Period of literature, horribly bad by any standard, still had to be covered, because it comes first. Students now are equipped with special talents in the ability to process **randomly.** The remote control device must have been tailor-made for random learners to skip, hop, and jump over one hundred channels. *Sesame Street* presents cartoon characters eating up a whole screen full of "g's" today, "x's" tomorrow. Just as family dinner time gave way to "grazing," sequential learning has given way to bits and bites caught on the fly. Learners fit these randomly digested pieces of information into a larger scheme constructed in their minds.

Ten years ago, students adjusted to a slow pace at school with reflection time built in. It commonly took an entire semester to teach *Moby Dick*—more time than it took for the United States to win the war in the Persian Gulf. Except for this more revered epic struggle between Ahab and the whale, the unit method of organizing curriculum typically resulted in six-week chunks of time. Now, the *Star Wars* trained generation has become attuned to **fast response.** Not only top guns in F18 Eagles respond instantaneously; even baby's first riding toy comes equipped with flashing lights, pop-up seat, whirligig ornament, and a siren or bell available at the push of a button. Baby's first ride is no longer simply a new stretching of muscles; it is a conditioning in visceral responses.

A View From the Mall

I am an educator…and I am afraid.

Close to my beat is an outdoor shopping center. One of the first in the nation. It used to have two department store anchors with an abundance of shoe stores. Now it has been transformed into a huge indoor mall with fewer shoes and more specialities. The entire bottom floor is one gigantic arcade. As shoppers take the down escalator, they see a fairyland of play.

Bangs and whistles and flashes and rat-a-tats assail the ears. Reds and yellows and greens fill the neon tubes. The panorama has a background black born of the machine casings in the studied darkness of the interior. The place is alive; the people do not speak. There, under the feet of strolling shoppers, is the "place," the natural habitat of today's youngsters.

From my food court advantage, my eyes follow a slogan-draped twelve-year-old with Mother's fortyish boyfriend going down the escalator for an interlude, while Mother sets out toward the center atrium. Luckily for me, the guys choose adjacent machines just within my view. I am struck by what I see.

The youngster, with Buffalo Bills' blue stripes running down the legs of his sweats, and his companion, with a number 32 football jersey, are poised at their machines. Buffalo slugs the machine. The asteroids implode into a black hole center and a cascade of alien transporters dart about. Buffalo's hands grip powerful laser beams of destruction. He flicks his interceptor about; the score display tallies faster and faster.

Number 32 worries the slug with his fingers. The screen scrolls an inviting scene. He watches, identifying the objects and reading the instructions at the bottom of the screen. They seem not to make sense to him since he looks even more puzzled when the display fades momentarily to black, then repeats itself.

Buffalo has reacted within an unknown environment, his mounting score marking his instant success, while Number 32 yet has not left the starting gate. He reflects and then reluctantly throws his slug in the slot.

Buffalo's hands are amazing. Instinctively, and simultaneously, they twist and push and thumb. The hands are guided by the sounds, the movements and the feel of the controls. Eyes seem to consume and deploy to the fingers in one great symphony. Mass destruction ensures.

Number 32 is overwhelmed by all the objects on the screen. The movement mesmerizes. Based on my own experiences, I know he is identifying all of the objects he sees, classifying them and running a verbal tape in his head to describe what role he is to play and what role each of the objects are to play while the game time passes.

Tentatively, his hands begin to move to the inaudible, but verbalized, directions sent by his mind. "Turn left with your right hand; a missile is approaching!" I can hear it all. His actions are sequenced. After a few errant sorties, his space ship falls in a lightening flash.

The slowly mounting score for Number 32 and the moderated advance of Buffalo's score stop abruptly as each is successful in his own way. As the two walk away, Number 32 starts to talk about the game; Buffalo absentmindedly watches passersby.

From two strange machines to two engaging experiences, learning has taken place.

There before me is the answer! I see a modern-day allegory of a concept educators have not yet perceived. Kids are different today. Not because of their clothes or their secret codes or their music. They are different today because of some basic physiological phenomena. Kids today react while the older generation reflects. They are random where we are sequential. They are holistic while we are linear. Their predominant sense is motion and touch whereas ours is hearing and seeing. As learners, they experience while we intellectualize.

My fear is that schools will not or cannot adjust to these differences in time. My fear is that we are using an excuse that kids don't want to learn when, in fact, they do. They just must learn differently.

The shift in learning patterns has been well-documented. Yet, the question of why is unresolved. It could be that these predilections are simply a matter of personal style and preference much like "Make my sundae hot fudge, please." Those educators who lean toward this rationale can find much support with the trend toward learning style assessments, personality type indicators, and the emerging appreciation for individual diversity within the classroom setting.

However, the preference causality is weakened when students become more and more incapable of flexibility in their learning acquisition styles. A generation ago, perhaps learners had style preferences, but were capable of learning in nonpreferential modes. Students sitting in the wooden chairs listening to a lecture may have been learning outside of their learning preference, yet with perseverance could learn anyway. Presumably those who were inflexible in style and, thus, could not adjust left school at an early age.

The evidence is mounting, however, that the fragility of the children of the 90s—their instability at home—their high anxiety in their day-to-day lives—render them incapable of learning style flexibility. It is no longer a hot fudge type preference. If this be the case, then schools will have to adjust to a "now" learning style or school must somehow teach learning style flexibility. When adjustments of any type are not made, success in school remains elusive for many children.

It could be that this shift in how children learn has an evolutionary basis. In *The Evolution of Consciousness*, Ornstein (1991) elaborates on the physiological changes of the brain over time. Since the brain was designed for changes to a higher order of functioning to occur over virtually millenniums, it stands to reason that no one single person or generation of people would be able to detect any perceptible change in brain structure. But one must reason, also, that in some perceivable time, someone, somewhere, should be able to notice. Certainly there must have been some point in time when an observer of culture would have concluded that man's brain had recessed from a prehistoric protruding forehead. Would there not be some generation that could observe that some tribes had brains capable of using tools, while another tribe nearby did not? Modern man no longer has such benchmarks of cultural evolution to higher order thinking so obvious as physical features or life changing capabilities. The changes in modern man are more subtle. It could be that our generation in the 1990s just may be at a point in time when physiological changes of humans have progressed to the point that we are the first ever generation to note the change.

It could be that the shift in learning processes is more a product of the adaptability of mankind as the pace of change accelerates, as our lives become engaged with higher and higher forms of technology, and as our value system expands to encompass more and more diversity. The troubling consternation over the probable effects of watching television could be an artifact of a new adaptability. Students of the 90s have been shaped by their environment. The differences in the way students approach learning may well be the result of this shaping.

Academicians may continue the *why* argument for many more decades, but educators do not have the luxury of waiting for the final conclusions. Schools that administer learning styles inventories to students conclude that more and more students exhibit learning styles counter to those historically relied upon by schools.

These differences in learning styles and the many changes that have taken place in the environment form the framework for a change imperative.

> **Students of the 90s have been shaped by their environment. The differences in the way students approach learning may well be the result of this shaping.**

Chapter Two

The Reasoned Imperative

Even the Queen Mary had to go to dry dock... Hardly a thing has escaped changing somewhat over time based on new technology or refined production techniques or change in aesthetic criteria. The can opener has gone from a punch of a knife blade, to a church key, to around-the-rim twisters, to a wall unit with a crank, to an electric grabber that whirls. Then came pop tops.

Even the perennial Christmas favorite, Barbie from Mattel, the ultimate "girl next door" has changed since March 1959, when she was introduced as an $11^1/_2$" fashion doll named Barbara Millicent Roberts. She started her life as a teenage model. Now more than three decades later, Barbie has transformed herself many times as she fulfills her creator's goal of mirroring the dreams, aspirations, and achievements of new generations of young women.

According to *Kaybee Goodtimes Magazine* (November/ December, 1992), Barbie's original Paris couture gave way to elegance inspired by Jacqueline Kennedy. She went "mod" with a face-lift in 1967. That lasted until the 70s when her smile was broadened and her hair streaked to reflect the beauty trends of the time. In total, Barbie has had more than 500 professional makeovers, knee joints in 1964, a twistable waist in 1967, and recently designed pivotal shoulders to go with her new luxurious hair. Her transformations have been more substantial than simply a case of fashion trend-chasing. Technology played an important role in her development. Lately, she appeared on retailers' shelves as an African-American, Hispanic, or Asian version to reflect cultural diversity.

"BARBIE"® doll ©1992 Mattel Inc.

Used with permission.

Only Superman existed without dry dock. However, Superman did emerge from his 1992 tomb with a noted style difference: Arnold Schwarzenegger's muscles, and hair longer and curlier than when he went in it.

If change is a natural part of life itself, it stands to reason that thinking, intelligent people immersed in their profession as educators could reason through why schools must change by using their intellect therefore forming a "reasoned" imperative for change. This "reasoned" imperative has resulted from new findings about the brain and humankind's physiological capability to learn.

Evolving from the mist that has shrouded the brain are current understandings that can be formulated into principles on how the brain functions. This new knowledge and the sound of more and more new knowledge to come means that schools can be organized and operated on the basis of principles of learning. The dawning of brain functioning should allow rituals of schooling to give way to principles of learning.

Now, operations and organizations of schools are based on schooling rituals or those traditions of how school ought to be. These rituals are passed from one generation's experience to another. These experiences are serving in lieu of knowledge, not unlike native American tribes who, lacking weather forecasting science, practiced rain dance rituals.

Or recall the summer ritual experience of virtually every child who was restrained to sit in a lawn chair under a big shade tree waiting the obligatory one hour after lunch before swimming. *Mom, can I go in yet? Canna huh? Please. How much longer? Now?* Lacking definitive knowledge, schools are encrusted with such rituals. These assumptions, which have become rituals of a sort, serve to preserve culture and define lines for education. These rituals remain pervasive and seldom examined in any meaningful way.

RITUALS OF SCHOOLING

1. Students will not learn without grades and other external motivators. Therefore, much energy at school and home is expended on grades and the issues that surround them such as grading periods and progress notes to alert parents before they are told what they will be told. A mystique has grown up around the grade book and the role it plays. It rarely comes in any color except black. It is sacred and cannot be read by others. It is the official recorder of learning that is stored in vaults for decades.

2. Human nature must be tamed to make productive future workers. Bells are needed to demand a switch of focus. This demand was a part of the preparation for the work culture of an industrial society as well as an efficiency tool for large schools with many students. Today, state of the art assembly lines that used to start with a bell and end with a bell are managed by the workers themselves in quality circles. Schools, however, still consider timeliness as a personal virtue; thus, tardy policies and the recording of infractions take teacher time and energy. Precise time frames when class ends (10:42 a.m.) reflect a ritual that schools should run like a metro train that just left the station. It is certainly possible to have no bells, no passing time, no change of classes, and no division of labor into subject matters, each with its own time demands, but….

3. What is to be learned is already agreed upon. This belief is grounded in decisions of the past rather than in a belief that those decisions were made by humans and can be subject to cancellation in favor of other decisions. Instead of a healthy dialogue on a continuous basis surrounding decisions about what is to be learned, the teacher's job is to preserve an inherently valued academic heritage.

4. Learning is a two step process—present something and test something in a falsely two-dimensional world. Educators presume a one-to-one ratio prevails in curriculum. For everything presented, there is one learning to master. Prevailing thought is that the purpose of schooling is to present knowledge and then test to ensure it is, indeed, known. The teacher's job is contained within well known parameters. Teachers' love of the certain segment of knowledge to be conveyed is the primary motivator for job satisfaction.

5. School serves a sorting function for society. The management of the academic knowledge to be conveyed and the orderly movement of students through the institution calls for a sorting of curriculum from hard to easy and a sorting of students from smart to dumb. Then, via the curriculum, the hard and smart are separated from the easy and dumb. The teacher's job becomes like that of a flour sifter. Sift the students, and sift the students, and sift them once more until what the teacher has to teach matches the right group of students. Society at large tolerates this sifting because students will be sorted before they reach the workplace. Those who make it through certain schooling levels can become elite while those who foundered on the shoals of schooling are the "other class." School plays a pivotal role in what Jonathan Kozol (1992) calls "savage inequalities." The sifting through schools gives rise to America's caste system. The sifting is accomplished through an interlocked self-perpetuating system of grades, levels by age, retention, and tracking by ability. A student must move through the system. Those who can't or won't, don't deserve further consideration.

> **How school operates, what teachers do, and what students do should be guided by known principles of learning.**

Given the lack of knowledge about learning, these beliefs about schooling served as organizational guidelines. Now that more knowledge exists about how learning takes place, the need for and the usefulness of such rituals as organizational strategies has passed. Rituals can now be assigned the exclusive preserve of social customs and mores that society wishes to be transmitted to the young. There is still a place for Friday night football, ceremonies, and rituals. But these rituals should not be the paradigm for school. The focus of school should be learning, not rituals of schooling.

The new paradigm should shift from *schooling* to *learning*. When such a shift of paradigm occurs, futurist Joel Barker claims that all systems return to zero; that is, all decisions are open for redeciding within a new context. How school operates, what teachers do, and what students do should be guided by known principles of learning.

NEWER PRINCIPLES OF LEARNING

Distillation of the expanding research on brain functioning can now yield just such a set of principles of learning to guide the organization and daily activity at school.

1. The brain responds to all the sensory environment, stimulating the "whole" of the person. All the neural pathways in the body light up like a pinball machine when the learner becomes engaged in learning. It is like sitting on the top row of the bleacher seats in a large gymnasium with a full-length view of the gym floor. The night before, a crew of people set up an enormous, yet intricate, maze of dominoes. There are side trails, simultaneous pathways; there are multiple focal points, and up, down, sideways, back and forth motions. The sterile gym floor has been turned into a synergistic creation of intricate connections, delicate but lasting. When the moment occurs, one simple touch of one finger initiates a whole floor full of happenings. The brain is like that initiator with a whole interactive organism at its disposal to mastermind a learning experience.

2. Our mature brain has been developed to play just such a central role. As children, we set up 28 dominoes because that is all that came in the box. We carefully placed them in one long row. The challenge was to get to the very last one in the line before a misguided motion prematurely sent them all to the ground with one *whish*. Dominoes akimbo were signs of connections unmade. However, when the 28 aligned properly, one touch of our child's finger sent them into rapid motion. But the connections were simple and strictly linear—a child's attempt to orchestrate a significant happening.

Perhaps educators have tried to make learning malleable to fit into just such a linear series of connections so that learning can be perceived as one forward thrust imprinting a pattern. Instead, physiologically, learning is more like a series of connectors among multiple motion pathways and mini-networks combining in unique ways to make gigantic imprints on a gigantic floor.

Implications of this principle in the classroom include designing activities that cause the brain to do many things at one time. For example, sources of information could be complex rather than simple. Lively social interaction group discoveries should be favored over a two-way information flow such as from teacher to student, worksheet to student, or film to student. An individual search on the part of students for information may result in lesser quality of information than the teacher could have provided. Nevertheless, student searches may be better because they stimulate multiple processing functions in the brain. Rather than reading *Cliff Notes* in preparation for a teacher lecture on Hawthorne's *The Scarlet Letter*, a student's time may be better spent selecting readings of their own choosing and writing their reactions in a personal journal. The book, self-selected by the student, may never reach the literary stature of a work of Hawthorne, but the learning that results from this type of activity is greater because it promotes multi-sensory experiences. The quality of learning should be judged by its richness, not by its efficiency.

3. The search for meaning is basic to the human being. Watching lower forms of animals who exhibit learning but do not have the benefit of "school" highlights the nature of learning. It seems we think that the only formal learning begins at six when children start school. Instead, the purpose of school should be to heighten and enhance the natural inclination of the human being to learn. This belief lessens the need to rely upon external motivators and control-oriented procedures that form such a central portion of the school experience for children and adults alike.

4. The brain understands and remembers best in spatial memory. Spatial memory is activated by an experience that draws on previous knowledge. Technology advances have allowed researchers to map activated centers in the brain as a person is exposed to learning stimuli. From the yield of these studies, an educator can now examine every activity to determine the degree

The quality of learning should be judged by its richness, not by its efficiency.

to which it is likely to be remembered and ready for further use in learning. Those activities that promote a first hand, authentic experience are likely to be remembered.

5. The brain does not function well under perceived threat. A student's experience at school should be perceived as high challenge yet low threat. The adage, "Talk softly but carry a big stick," should have no place in schools. Instead, a spirit of mutual cooperation within a supportive environment can be created where adults and students engage in mutually beneficial activity. An atmosphere without distress is one in which students and teachers respond with sensitivity and flexibility in a spontaneous way rather than in a matter-of-fact, task-oriented, routine manner. The hierarchical, teacher controlled management system must give way to an environment where status and responsibility are delegated to students and monitored by the teachers. The concept that a portion of the teacher's responsibility is to dole out punishment for rule infractions with a purpose of promoting self-discipline in the young is counterproductive to learning.

6. Each brain is unique; therefore, there should be choices. It is exceedingly presumptuous for educators to think that only we have the professional knowledge and training to determine suitable learning activities. Concepts such as 1) teaching to the middle, 2) some will get it; some won't, and 3) the responsibility for learning belongs to the student are archaic. Students should be offered choices so that they can accommodate their own uniqueness—uniqueness of learning style—uniqueness of background—uniqueness of perceived goals.

> Students should be offered choices so that they can accommodate their own uniqueness—uniqueness of learning style, background, and perceived goals.

7. The brain resists meaningless patterns imposed on it. Teachers' selection of isolated pieces of unrelated information should yield to activities and information sources that students, themselves, can fit into a pattern. For students, then, learning becomes a search for meaning within the framework of concepts, and relationships, and pattern matching.

These principles represent new understandings that educators have gleaned from current brain research centered in the medical community. Medical researchers have been studying the brain for decades, going back to the split brain research of the 1940s. New technology such as CAT scans and MRI's (Magnetic Resonance Imaging) have accelerated revelations of how the brain makes human beings what they are. Educators have not been active in researching the physiological side of "learning," leaving that field to medicine. Even if educators were not the primary researchers, we can at least apply learning principles. Efforts to maintain schooling rituals could be more productively turned toward dialogue, experimentation, and extension of creating schools based on learning principles. As Marzano (1988) emphasizes, every teacher should become an expert on learning and use that knowledge as an imperative for reasoned change, aligning and integrating curriculum while reframing the way teachers teach and students learn.

Chapter Three

The Direction of Change

To "The Change Imperative" and "The Reasoned Imperative" (Chapters One and Two) must be added an overriding call for change. The purpose of education itself has changed. It is as though one were a highly skilled baseball player, the likes of masterful Cardinals Ozzie Smith or Lou Brock. With stolen base records accumulated at an amazing rate and the ability to be lead-off hitters, season after season, these All-Star players knew the art of the game of baseball.

What if, in their thirteenth season, they entered the locker room only to hear their manager announce, "The Commissioner has determined that from this day forward, the goal of each game is to help the other team win."

Likewise, the purpose of education has changed. In whatever phraseology one prefers, the purpose of education always has been primarily to acquire knowledge. Now, in the shadow of a new century, there is too much knowledge, old and new, for one to "acquire" it.

The central goal of acquiring knowledge has bound together all groups across ages throughout diversities. It no longer serves. The purpose of education must change to engaging students in searching for meaning. Schools, classrooms, and teachers must be transformed into learning communities whose purpose is to provide for learners significant experiences that the brain can recognize, organize, and apply. The teachers of the learning community orchestrate rich experiences and help students in their search for meaning.

This fundamental shift in purpose presents large landscapes for change that require new architectures to form a framework for what teachers teach and what students learn. Architecture has long been a term used to denote the framework or design of structures. Others then follow this design to make decisions about what the final structure will be—what it will contain, in what sequence it should be constructed, what workers will use which places within the structure. If it were not for the "art" of architecture, all creations for humankind to inhabit might look like Freddie The Freeloader's habitat. In that abomination of helter-skelter boxes, Red Skelton could mime his way into our hearts. But Freddie's life, carried out absent from an overall framework or creation of purpose, lacked a plan. Freddie's was a life gone awry with no framework, no architecture. Lest it go awry, curriculum too must have a grand design, a framework, an architecture within which educators may formulate their plans to guide searches for purpose.

In this turbulence of change, some educators reach out, seeking some road map to follow. Others seek shelter to ward off changes. Neither seekers' nor hiders' positions are tenable. The hiders will one day have to emerge from hibernation to peek at the outside. They will be unable to see, because their sight will have failed. The seekers face a far different fate. Volleys from the right and salvos from the left leave seekers caught in a cross fire. The list of combatants is long: policymakers, legislators, elected officials, parents, teachers, boards of education, while a similarly long list identifies those who have a plan to make schools better.

Caught in the middle of multiple leaders gathering legions of followers, seekers struggle to find a personal position.

All of the reform movements, from wholesale change at the state level in Kentucky to a school-by-school coalition approach such as Ted Sizer's (1992), are rolling along one right after another. They gain momentum as the ultimate solutions to educators who are dismayed at public outcries and frustrated by their own lack of success in teaching the youngsters of the 90s. To bring clarity to the confusing reform efforts, one can put reforms into four categories named for the motivations of its proponents. It is helpful to categorize the various reform efforts by their essential characteristic—or by their "R Factor."

PENDULUM BASHING

Pendulums have got to go.

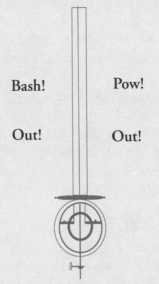

Bash!   Pow!

Out!   Out!

We no longer have room in education for such thoughts.
The pendulum is a horrific metaphor for the change process.
A pendulum is mindless.
It is mechanistic.
It is impervious to its environment.
It is fatalistic.
It can only cut the same grooves.
It may run clocks well, but with digitals, even that is in doubt. It certainly does no good for us educators.

With over 10 years of reform movement experience, we should be able to synthesize the characteristics of change better than that. I, at least, don't want to look back ten years ago and conclude that I have returned to where I started. How depressing! How I know that that cannot possibly be true! I am not the same. I know things now I didn't know, could not possibly have known, then.

I will either figure out a better way to explain what is going on, or I will just continue to stubbornly reject this old pendulum saw. Being an educated person, I will try the figuring out route first.

Think of water running down a stream…just a little trickle, not a mighty flood. It runs and runs downhill peeking into crevices and eddying into little back washes. It is so fluid that it spills all over. If one places a concrete block in its way, it seeps and seeps until it reaches its furthest outer boundaries. Then it begins to fold back on itself, making a mini top current and a bottom current until it reaches the mainstream. It may now carry a leaf acquired in some eddy. It may have absorbed some mineral as it filled the crevice.

The water that has reached its limit and returns is not the same property it was. In reaching for some outer limit, it "learned" some things, or picked up some things. When the outer limit sends it coursing back, it cannot be the same. Water does not mindlessly flow back and forth, going from an outer limit on one side of the stream to the outer limit on the other side of the stream. The fact that it is in the act of flowing itself denotes movement, not stagnation.

I believe that the progress of education is like a water flow. We head in one direction for awhile until we reach an outer limit, a barrier. Then, just as fluid, we are rather abruptly turned in another direction and it may seem as though we are going back where we just came from. However, we have changed in the process of reaching out to an outer limit. We have changed; therefore what looks like a simple return to an earlier origin is in fact a far different phenomenon. It is indeed a most substantial change.

The Four Categories of Reform Efforts

1. Revolutionaries

Many calls for reform attempt to make radical structural changes in schools. Ted Sizer's coalition outlines nine essential characteristics that he claims will revolutionize schooling. Chicago schools took a giant, yet errant, revolutionary step in school governance by putting the school in the hands of the public. This movement since has been declared unlawful. In the East, Boston schools were turned over to a university for operation. Word has it that that is not working well either. Private enterprise has entered the picture with various Kentucky Colonels all claiming the ability to concoct a better batter. The Bush "America 2000" and now Clinton "Goal 2000" movement is deeply rooted in just such a revolutionary spirit, albeit overlaid by a more conservative effort to meet politically acceptable national goals. All of these reforms share a "break-the-mold" quality. The hope is that through radical departure from past structure, schools will be more effective.

To be revolutionary, one must throw out common wisdom in favor of new organizational principles that call for different individual behavior within given organizational parameters. History has taught that radical reform of governments most readily occurs by revolution, or a shooting war. Today's revolutionaries have declared a war without bullets.

2. Revisionists

A significant number of educators are promoting change by revising various elements of a school's program. Reading-writing workshops are fast taking over the field of remedial reading, taught by specialists. Math through manipulatives has superseded textbook story problems. Whole language approaches have relegated the basal reader to a lonely spot on the bookshelf. Even the national associations of various academic areas have set new agendas, each changing its own component of the overall mixture that serves as school curriculum. Revisional types of changes are the most researched of all change movements with statistical backing for claims of more success than provided by old methodology. These revisions are easier to implement than revolutionary reforms because the change impacts only a single element of school, not the school itself. Therefore, revisionists fall short of systemic change.

One of the major outcomes of World War II was the field of systems analysis. "D Day," an unparalleled landing of gigantic forces on a foreign shore, is attributed to military planners who divided the invasion into its operational parts. There was the supply line; the tank war; the assault troops; the air support. By detailing these essential elements and fitting them into a cohesive plan, the planners created an invasion that still stands as a benchmark of strategical planning. Likewise, revisionists see school as one big system that can be changed by tinkering with its individual component parts. In this tinkering, revisionists frequently lose sight of the overall picture, and therefore stumble when far-reaching change is needed.

3. Reductionists

Another sector of reformists takes an altogether different approach. Reductionists are those who believe that schools would be more successful if the content to be learned were only broken down into discrete bits of knowledge. In this fashion, teachers would know exactly what content to present. Tests could be designed to cover only that content specifically taught. Hence, mastery learning as a conceptual base for schooling took root. State departments of education found this view of schooling well-suited for their goal of standardizing education across diverse school districts within their area of supervision. Reductionists also can produce key skills and core competency lists that can be adopted statewide with textbooks keyed to those identified discrete bits of knowledge.

The reductionists believe that schools can benefit from such systematic systems because these systems make logical sense. The problem is that the human brain learns in ways other than those that make perfect logical sense. Additionally, the challenges that face the student of the 21st century cannot be foretold. If known discrete knowledge and skills are all that are learned, reductionists are already outmoded by the time their curriculums and lists of competencies are published. Reductionists can feel good about their change efforts because the changes are very explainable and very visible; yet one can question their definition of education with the criticism that it looks more like training, than learning.

4. Reactionaries

Heated debate on the purpose of schooling and the content to be used comes from a quarter that affiliates with the religious and political right wings. Their philosophy is forged in the past with a long and noble history, beginning with McGuffey readers. McGuffey presented the alphabet illustrated by Bible passages. Reactionaries wish to return education to the way it used to be, or at least to a romanticized version of the way it has always existed in the public's mind. Both from national platforms and from local activism, the reactionaries bring heated controversy as a style of change.

The reactionaries have been successful in a political sense, accomplishing the reduction of federal aid to education in dollar value. Reagan's Department of Education under Secretary Bennett had a conservative bent. A classical education was promoted with attempts to distribute government funds under "choice" programs.

Their perspective on classical education with conservative values offers an alternative to liberal educators. Their counter-point to the public debate has added to the noise but has not resulted in sweeping reforms acceptable to the mainstream.

If the revolutionaries got stuck on structure and met with hard-line resistance from teachers faithful to their content; if revisionists have changed parts but have not seen the synchronization of the school as a whole; if the reductionists have built an unreal picture of what education is, albeit an efficient one; if the reactionaries fan ideological storms that put restraints on change rather than promote change; if all of these "R factors" are the array of change alternatives, then current efforts to change will fail.

If the "ultimate" solution is not any of the "R factors," then a more congruent descriptor for the nature of change is needed.

Considering the change imperative and the reasoned imperative, a transformational change is called for. A transformational change implies that what was one form will alter itself to become something new, something that did not exist before. In transformation the origin of the new can be found in the old form. But the old loses its form in favor of the new structure which creates a new being. For a school to experience transformational change, it would little resemble its former self, in form or in function. Its very architecture would be new.

Examples of transformational change in nature are numerous. The tadpole becomes a frog, the caterpillar becomes a butterfly, water becomes steam. In organizational terms, however, transformational change is rare. Companies and groups more often die than prevail through such change. The mom and pop grocery store, the family doctor who made house visits, the man who repaired cars in his home-built garage—all of these found themselves obsolete. Those who had the ability to transform themselves survived as supermarket managers, hospital-bound specialists, manufacturer-trained technicians. There are those who transform and those whose culture dies.

The geopolitical struggles of the 90s are transformations in process. It is yet to be seen what world map and world alliances will emerge from the transformation process.

Schools are poised as at the beginning of a transformational change that will touch every practice, every ritual, every custom, every person within it. No lesser extent of change will suffice.

Transformational change accomplished so easily in nature apparently is very difficult within the context of people and their job behaviors. John Goodlad (1984) has been about transformational change of schools since the early 60s. In a small paragraph in the last chapter of *Horace's School*, Ted Sizer (1992) alludes to having run into a juggernaut. In some senses, there is a tremendous gulf between the 200 schools recognized each year as blue ribbon schools and the hundreds of schools that could never qualify as examples of excellence. Transformational change is hard.

METAPHORS

Part of this difficulty is explainable, but it takes a small side journey to the land of the metaphoric mind. A human's brain is organized around metaphors. Instead of every action, belief or value being a product of a specific, learned reaction, the mind establishes parallels. For example, a female who sees herself as a mother carries within her the metaphor of *mother*. Not every motherly act must be specifically learned; instead, the metaphor of a mother has been embedded in the metaphoric mind. The human mind uses many metaphors. Throughout the ages, common metaphors remain embedded and thus, unexamined. However the inculturation happens, the metaphor surrounding the role of *teacher* is embedded also.

The metaphor of *teacher* may take one of several forms within any one person's perception. A common metaphor is that a teacher is like a pitcher filled with life-sustaining water. The glasses arrayed near the pitcher are void of content—empty glasses. The act of teaching is like pouring from a teacher's full pitcher, filling the students' empty glasses. This metaphor results in behaviors like lecturing, positioning the teacher in front of a fairly large number of students who are seated below the teacher's position. This metaphor implies that there is only one source of knowledge and that knowledge must be imparted in equal measure to all.

Another metaphor goes under the name of *Tabula Rasa*. The purpose of the teacher is to inscribe the wisdom of the ages upon those who are considered blank slates. Teachers whose metaphor is drawn from this philosophy would see themselves as all knowing in a mystical sense with a mission to inscribe sacred knowledge upon the innocent.

Teachers whose actions are based on this metaphor feel *knighted,* or the modern word is *empowered,* in a noble sense to gather children unto the bosom of the ages. These teachers have about them a righteousness and an indisputable hold on what children need to learn.

Other teachers act as *shepherds* protecting their flock.

A commonality among these metaphors is that they are so deeply embedded that the person acts from these beliefs without awareness of the underlying values contained within his/her own perceived metaphor. Embedded metaphors make transformational change difficult, because these metaphors are from the old form and do not have the richness of any newer form.

A New Metaphor is Needed

A metaphor for the new century should 1) encompass the nature of today's children, 2) recognize the change in the purpose of education, and 3) embrace a new way of teacher-to-student interaction that will heighten students' engagement in constructing meaning. Such a metaphor has been needed for ten years. None has been forthcoming although asking workshop participants to reveal their own metaphor for teaching and learning has become common. These spur-of-the-moment writings are more reflective of a communications exercise than representative of a fundamental change in teachers' beliefs about themselves. A key component of a modern metaphor must include the adult's discovering the context in which a student lives as well as drawing students into a world wider than they experience directly.

Let's call the new metaphor *entrancing,* taken from the word *enter* which connotes a person taking an initiative step toward something still yet to be revealed. With its *ing* ending, the word retains a sense of continuous motion.

Enter the child's world

A bank of shouting media types corners the 1992 Olympians from the "Dream Team," the most awesome concentration of basketball court talent ever assembled. Moreover, this talent pool is probably the greatest ever assembled in any sport in the whole of Olympic history. The questions from the shouting reporters' group come rapid fire to the talent group. One question goes to Magic Johnson, who answers in a soft voice. Another question goes to Larry Bird. In ping pong fashion, the press conference continues. Having exhausted any salient questions in the early moments of the conference, the reporters' questions begin to drift into mediocrity until a pivotal moment occurs. To Charles Barkley, one reporter asks, "How did you feel when the U.S.A. team lost the Gold to the Soviets in 1970?" His serious reply is, "Well, I don't know, because I was in kindergarten."

How easily adults lose the context of the younger generation.

Adjusting to generational change is hard. Consider only a generation back when traveling meant following the old Route 66 winding from the Midwest through the Rockies to desert, finally ending in the golden land. The journey was rich with encounters, with two pump gas stations fronted by stucco pillars separating the outside pumps with no roof from the drive-through pumps close to the building. Or a mixture of dread laced with anticipation at opening the door of a tiny motel room where the father preceded the family to preview the room to make sure it was clean. This was long before the days of Holiday Inns. In the 40s generation, the cafes were likely to be named "Mom's" or were identified by a neon sign flashing "Eat." In these very small enterprises, one could always find a hamburger of unknown quality. Just a generation ago.

If this generational change scenario leaves one shaking the head in awe, how even more difficult it is to understand the context of a student's life when the pace of change has accelerated to every five years instead of generation by generation.

Now, the children of the 90s cross the country by jet with no feel of the land speeding by unseen beneath them. Even car journeys are a matter of simple steering over multi-lane strips of never ending concrete. No reflective green sign announces a neon "Eat" or a one man filling station. Instead, such a sign announces the presence of McDonalds or Burger King or Hardees known by every American to be places where quality has been standardized. The context of traveling has changed. Changed from hamburgers of unknown quality to an Arizona burger that tastes exactly like a Mississippi one.

A counselor tells this story. She is working at her desk one day when a teacher with kid in tow heads for a phone call awaiting her in the main office.

"Can I leave Otis here for a little while? I'll just be a minute."

With that, the counselor gestures at a side chair next to the desk for Otis to be seated. Glancing at his angry face, she decides not to say anything but lets him initiate interaction. He soon becomes bored with the silence and begins to look around the small cubicle that has a collection of pictures and other memorabilia with personal meaning to her. When his eyes stop their wandering, he focuses on a watercolor of the Lincoln Memorial in Washington D. C. from the vantage point of the reflective pool.

"What's that?" he asks.

"That's the Lincoln Memorial," she says. "That's my most favorite place in Washington D.C. I go there every chance I get. You can walk up those large steps there and see the statue of Lincoln."

"Is he really in there?" Otis asks.

"Oh, no, she hastily retreats; "Lincoln is not really in there; it's his statue."

Tentatively Otis wonders, "Is he alive?"

"Not alive."

"How did he die?"

Frantically, she hopes the right answer will pop into her mind from some long unused deep recess of her memory.

"Oh yeah, someone shot him."

Then she begins to finish writing on some work that had been interrupted by this exchange, thinking the conversation will come to an end. But no.

"Who shot him?"

Oh, memory do not fail this time either. "John . . . ," then in a rush, "John Wilkes Booth."

"Where is he now? Is he in jail?"

(Does this conversation never end.) "He's buried."

Before the young man could continue, she gives the classic body language of disengagement by turning her chair away.

In reflection, she realized that the context of Otis' life did not include such things as statues and memorials and Washington D.C. historical presidencies, all knowledge that adults think is common. Otis had no concept of honor that is bestowed by building statues. His sense of time had no perspective; there was only now. Far better, she concluded, would be to have entered his world by finding out how he would honor someone close to him who has died. Could there be some way to listen to him talk about those who are heroes to him? Were they to die, what physical manifestation of their life would he build to leave something of themselves?

She later found out there were parallels in his world. Otis's brother was killed in a drive-by shooting.

A loss of context.

The new metaphor begins with teachers entering the children's world as contrasted to seeing themselves as explaining adult things to help children become adults faster. Some educational psychologists would call this stage "determining what is developmentally appropriate." Because we have lost the context of children's lives, we have to learn that context before we can make any judgment about appropriateness. When context is lost, meaning is lost. To regain meaning, a new context must be perceived. Teachers can gain this perception by interacting with a child about his view of his world.

When context is lost, meaning is lost. To regain meaning, a new context must be perceived.

33

Exploring the child's world

Enter a fun house in the carnival that periodically makes its rounds. A room of mirrors is a must. For the less adventurous or for the stingy, usually a sample mirror is displayed outside the door. One does not have to go in if one does not want to. But who could pass by without a surreptitious glance at a body made bizarre? Inside the room is multiple bizarreness!

Sometimes, once adults enter a child's world, they will discover that the child's world is bizarre in many aspects. In a child's world, a statue can be alive. In a child's world, there can be imaginary friends. In a child's world, there can be friends who in the child's view, taunt. In a young teen's life, all the world stares at them. These are not misperceptions of the unknowing, but real substance of a youngster's life. After entering this world and perhaps discovering some strange perceptions, adults can ask students to explain their world. Who are these people? Why would they want to persecute? What makes the youngster think the world is staring?

One can expect that the child's world will be made up of these perceptions which are a part of growing up. But also there will be found contexts that adults cannot imagine. What do you do when you are hungry and there is no food? How could a child have been given away to someone else? What would be the adjective youngsters would use to describe the safety of their world when they are picked up at school at five p.m., when their school closes at two? How could one imagine a conversation between a mother and a fourteen year old daughter in a hospital room the day after they have both given birth.

Before teachers can make decisions about suitable learning experiences, they must reconnect with the context of students by designing interactions that allow students to make known, perhaps for the first time, their analyses of their own world.

Introduce students to the adult world

Gently. Ever so gently. Children need to be introduced to the adult world. Information, new perspectives, ideas honed in a forum of peers all help youngsters reshape the landscape of their own world. Their new understandings, gained through engaging in activity with an adult learning guide, help them grow in developmentally appropriate ways. Far from being Rousseau's child and left to grow up naturally, today's child benefits from learning about the adult world and applying it to his own world. Where there are differences, congruence can be created; where there are inaccuracies, new knowledge can emerge; where there are misconceptions, the ability to interpret more accurately can grow. This shaping, which students do to their own world, is a different process than that which occurs when a teacher drills students on right responses.

In this adult world element of the new metaphor, teachers will be the most comfortable because it most resembles what they have defined their job to be all along. The adult world is full of information flow, activities completed, papers written, videos viewed, computers activated, experiments initiated. However, the *genesis* of an activity is a joint judgment born of juxtaposing different contexts, one of the adult and one of the child. A teacher who understands a particular child's world can better respond to a child's entry in a response journal that describes a home scene unlike any the teacher has ever experienced or imagined. Interactions between the teacher and the student can occur on an equal basis when the teacher understands the student's world. Unfortunately, it is the teacher's responsibility to bend so as to incorporate the child's world into the everyday workings at school because students are not developmentally able to encompass an adult world within their own. From this dissonance between worlds comes the students' perception that school work has no relationship to their lives but instead is born of an adult need to control the child's life, replacing the child's perceptions with ones more acceptable to adults. Learning can become more authentic as it becomes grounded in the consciousness of the learner.

Work in that world
The fourth element of the *entrancing* metaphor is to help the student work in an adult world. Those students whose learning style is mainly kinesthetic and tactile, those who are task-oriented, will be able to apply what is learned in this third stage. It is in this

Learning can become more authentic as it becomes grounded in the consciousness of the learner.

stage that students can involve themselves in projects and products reflecting their new understandings. Self-esteem and personal responsibility can come to center stage as students experience the feeling of being engaged in meaningful, productive work.

The whole of school should be analogous to the real life that occurs outside school walls.

As more and more students come from poverty levels, they may have few adult role models who engage in productive work. A common criticism is that American society has promoted generations of welfare families who never hold an expectation of work. Schools could help break that chain. Students should build, create, construct, accomplish, and feel the satisfaction that comes from completing a worthwhile task well. Only in modern times have schools removed themselves from the arena of productive working lives. The whole of school should be analogous to the real life that occurs outside school walls.

In this fourth stage, teachers can set up experiences that are real to students stemming from their view of their own world and enriched by the new knowledge of the adult world.

SEARCHING FOR MEANING

The final dimension of the *entrancing* metaphor occurs when learners reach out to the rest of society in ways that allow them to become a meaningful part of the larger society. Here, the projects worked on can be extended outside the school walls to a larger community than just a class of students. First, students must define who the larger community is in the context of what they have created. The larger community could well be fellow classmates in another part of the school, or in another grade. A larger community could be a neighborhood, or could be the student's own family grouping. Perhaps it could be organizations within the larger society. Reaching out may take the form of ecological movements, support of community organizations, or the causes and missions that make America a country of forever frontiers. The first stages of the metaphor are the kicks that propel a student in a forward motion to this last stage of involvement that enriches all of us even as students are enriched by their own actions.

***Entrancing* as metaphor has the power to change teachers' behavior who in turn open up the school system for transformational change.**

In its extreme, *entrancing* would dictate that every student's school experience may need to be different. Yet to be seen is just how far the educational system is able to extend and enlarge itself in replacing *schooling* with *learning* through a new embedded metaphor.

Chapter Four

Architecture

The central organizing determinant of the school should be the curriculum. Historically, many other facets of school life have played the central role. In fact, so seldom has the focus been on curriculum that many schools have no way of discussing the issues surrounding the curriculum. Conversation and problem-solving are more likely to be about procedures, policies, rituals, rules, mores, and customs. Consider the "hot topics" of typical faculty discourse:

When should we schedule parent conferences?

What criteria should be used for retention?

How should the parent organization's money be distributed?

Which students should not be allowed to go on a field trip?

How can we schedule more team planning time?

Which students should be given priority in the computer lab?

Do counselors or teachers make phone calls home?

In which portions of the learning disabilities diagnostic process should teachers be involved?

Who should run the National Jr. Honor Society's food drive?

How can lunch room supervision be minimized?

What should we do to discipline students who are tardy?

Why shouldn't parents be made to come to school to pick up report cards?

Even if all these concerns were to have admirable resolutions, the course of a student's academic life would remain essentially untouched. The access of a student to meaningful learning would not have been altered. Whatever was happening to students before these resolutions still would be happening after them.

Those middle schools whose central organizing determinant is the curriculum have a far different level of concern, one that is higher in intensity and in a moral dimension than schools who run on rituals.

Consider these scenarios:

School A: The central organizing principle here is accumulating credits, which are equated with time spent. The curriculum is organized around bodies of time. When enough credit is garnered, graduation occurs. Penalties and rewards are bestowed for those who do not get enough credit and for those who get too much credit.

School B: The central organizing principle in this school is the academic program organized by subject areas. So subject specialists are hired. They alone determine what the curriculum becomes. In most cases, the curriculum is almost indistinguishable from the person who delivers it.

School C: The central organizing principle here is the competency of teachers. Classes are offered in the areas in which teachers have certification. The school program is essentially what the faculty is prepared to teach.

If the curriculum itself were the central organizing principle, the important "talk" of school would be:

What is developmentally appropriate?

What student needs must be provided for?

How do students learn?

Can equity of access be increased?

What is the quality of decisions made on students' behalf?

It is clear that those middle schools whose central organizing principle is the curriculum have a far different level of concern, one that is higher in intensity and in a moral dimension than schools who run on rituals. As Polite (1992) concluded in her description of an exemplary middle school:

What makes a school exemplary is not the answers it has to all of the questions, but that the questions are being asked… it is the school's willingness to confront the difficult issues, to struggle with the problems because they are recognized, to see what most schools chose to ignore . . . it is, in the end, the school's ability to look in the mirror to see what is there; to meet the reflection with honesty; if what is seen is not what is desired, to act purposefully to change it. (p. 3)

As she concludes her findings, Polite highlights one school that has struggled to make curriculum the central organizing principle. She describes its signature as one of "pervasive tension born of challenges to conventional thought and practice and battles within a culture in metamorphosis."

When the focus is on curriculum, the center stage is staked out by what teachers are to teach and students are to learn. In contrast, if the central organizing principle were instruction, center stage would be claimed by the most effective presentation methods.

For too long an almost immutable curriculum has been left squarely in the middle between the teacher and the student. It has squatted there for decades until it has begun to rot away, smelling like grandma's greens. If it were to be opened up to the fresh air of reasoned examination, the fighting would begin in earnest.

Who is to control the curriculum?

Who should lead the reconsideration efforts?

What happens to all the other rituals and customs that are now removed from center stage?

Who determines the underlying values?

No one wants to touch these issues, because they lead right to the heart of how a school is run and what teachers are to do in it. Tenure laws, certification requirements, adopted textbooks, Carnegie units, and pressures from higher levels of education have managed to keep curriculum in the shadowy wings rather than in the revealing light of center stage.

For all these reasons, curriculum has been a spectator in its own sport. For curriculum to take its rightful place, a widely accepted definition of what it is and what it is not needs to be formulated.

Everyone knows a circle imprinted with a picture of a cigarette marked with a diagonal line drawn through it means "No Smoking."

Likewise, similar signs could be designed depicting the areas that have been mistaken as curriculum.

Defining curriculum

Authors of education texts have a field day defining curriculum. The definitions vary widely, although they usually define curriculum as more than the combined courses of study. In many ways it may be more helpful to start here by defining what curriculum is *not*.

The curriculum is not a collection of textbooks. A teacher who perceives curriculum as books is controlled by company authors who predetermine the value of certain information at the time of publication. They limit the world of learning solely to reported knowledge. Curriculum is then seen as the dissemination of selected information which may or may not be of consequence to the learner.

The curriculum is not revision. Some believe that curriculum development is the two weeks in the summer when revision is completed—a time to redo handouts, print additional copies, make a new overhead when the old ones are cracked and stained by age; but not a time to make major new decisions. These are the people who approach the new photocopying machine with a fist full of purple dittos to run off, not even accommodating the technical change. Dittos haven't been used since the 70s.

The curriculum is not a sequenced list of skills and competencies. "Since testing occurs in the spring, I've got to cover this material by the end of the first semester," commented one such believer. If one places check marks beside those competencies already "covered," the curriculum becomes the unchecked boxes.

The curriculum is not a course guide of prerequisites and course titles. Some groups' responses to defining curriculum are that curriculum consists of those activities planned to prepare students for the next level. It seems that no grade level has worth in and of itself except as it prepares students for the next level. Some teachers hired for summer work to prepare curriculum think their job is done when they have decided to eliminate one course and edit the course catalog.

The curriculum is not scope and sequence. Scope and sequence are agreements made in the context of a large committee, departmental groupings or state departments regarding content and calendars. When charged with curriculum development, these believers print a new wall chart.

The curriculum is not the teacher's preference. Computers become an end rather than a means when a science teacher begins an advanced degree in computer science. A school becomes known for its percussion group when that is the primary skill the band director possesses.

Before one can affect curricular change, one must be perfectly clear about what curriculum is as well as what it is not.

Curriculum is a plan to engage students in learning. These words suggest that curriculum is a set of decisions that planners make about how to access resources, activities, facilities, previous experience, and make connections with other learnings. Planners may be teachers, students, or a combination of the two. The quality of the plan is measured by how well students can engage in learning by being involved in carrying out the plan.

Creating a curriculum architecture

To create a quality plan, attention must be paid to its architecture, or the ordered arrangement of the parts of the system. The parts the plan must encompass include how teachers are deployed, what content will be called for, through what process, to which groups of students, for how long, and where they are in congruence with the values held in high esteem by the planners. In the creative overall design curriculum becomes the organizing principle.

Following are three examples of schools that have created unique curriculum designs. While they differ, all make evident the fact that planning proceeded from the notion that curriculum should evolve from the learner not the school or the teacher.

1. In **Brown-Barge,** a magnet middle school in Pensacola, Florida, the faculty created a curriculum architecture that serves as the organizing principle of their school. The story: a school committee visited another middle school on a quest to find ideas for their school. From their visit, the committee sensed the concept of curriculum architecture even though it was not a conscious awareness on their part. At the airport waiting for their return flight, the group, in an almost natural progression, began to create the framework for a new curriculum, a new plan of access to learning for students. They began to think about curriculum as "stream themes."

They conjectured that their staff could write streams that would cover most needs and concerns of their young adolescent population as well as their parent constituency. They further posited that every stream, although varied in detail or content, would contain three "learning tiers." Their concept was that within a theme students could progress through the tiers that all had a flexible schedule, cross grade level structures, and planned student interaction time.

At Brown-Barge, the *Acquisition Tier* is designed for basic skills necessary for success in all streams. Some students may acquire these skills separately while others will acquire them concurrently within the second tier of application.

The *Application Tier* within each stream consists of content drawn from any subject area which supports the stream. The third tier of *Simulation* is the creative culmination of learning where "real life" activities come into play. Within this basic framework, other typical middle school issues such as plant design, evaluation of student performance, and utilization of technology could be addressed.

Curriculum architecture usually can be reflected in a logo-like design such as the Brown Barge Triangle. A curricular architecture also can be reflected in a school schedule although this method of visualization is a little more dangerous. It is too easy to be misunderstood. Note, however, that even though its manifestation may be in a schedule, curriculum architecture relates to the curricular program, not scheduling. Scheduling is putting bodies in spaces. Program is the relationship of the concepts to the people in time and in space.

2. **Holman Elementary School** in St. Louis County is another school that acknowledged its need for a "make-over." The school sought assistance from the RJR Nabisco Foundation through its Next Century Schools program. This effort resulted in their designing a new curriculum architecture for their school that had embedded within it their most earnest dreams of what a school for their youngsters should be.

They conceived a plan of access anchored by small, family-like groups of one adult and eight children of various ages. They then thought anew and reached consensus on learning outcomes of National Standards quality. The small family groups would pursue attaining these outcomes in learning centers. Each learning center would contain a high technology environment connected by broad human themes such as *communication* or *inquiry*. Within the school day, a student sometimes would be in the center with the family. At other times, the same student could engage in learning in a center with a cohort group.

Once this framework was designed, Holman scoped out a total community services dimension from basic health service to overnight shelters, to family therapy, to adult retraining for its troubled neighborhood.

Holman's architecture is apparent in what is called Holman's Change Matrix.

Holman's Change Matrix

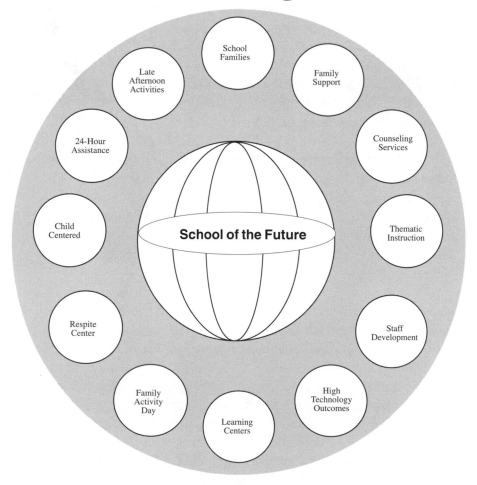

To Transform Education

3. **Cross Keys Middle School** has designed its curricular architecture twice in its eight-year transformation efforts. Its first design, used on an experimental basis, featured dividing the curriculum into a humanities strand and a technical strand. The humanities strand consisted of the traditional subjects of English, social studies, art, and foreign language while the technical strand contained mathematics, science, industrial arts, and home economics.

The students were randomly assigned at the first of the year to one of these strands, changing to the opposite strand the next quarter. This framework meant that students had longer concentrations of time in fewer subjects with fewer teachers and, conversely, longer periods of time without the subjects in the alternative strand.

Although not much change occurred in instructional delivery or content, this architecture did promote a healthier student attitude toward school according to the school's formal evaluation results.

At a later stage in their transformation process, the Cross Keys' staff agreed to a new architecture that accommodated student learning styles and promoted total integration of learning outside the confines of academic subject areas. This architecture moved the school past structural change into the substance of curriculum.

Teams of teachers planned units around a central concept, deemed essential. This concept was then explicated through activities that accommodated student learning styles. Each unit tended to be about 15 days long. In this fashion, students were engaged in their preferential style for at least one fourth of the time while being introduced to and taught to be accommodating of the different learning styles of other students.

In another dimension, the architecture was guided by a five step teaching process that actualized the metaphor explained in Chapter 3:

1. Entering the child's world
2. Exploring that world
3. Introducing the adult world
4. Working in that world
5. Searching for meaning

This multifaceted design, or plan of access, we believe, is congruent with current thought and is philosophically sound.

Cross Keys' architecture played out in their logo of a space age pinwheel. In an interesting variation, a segment of the pinwheel appears as a stylized space ship which now identifies their materials and is reproduced on their school stationery. Teams found that this architecture allowed a great deal of freedom to select new content. The new architecture provided a framework within which teams could make decisions together with less vested interest.

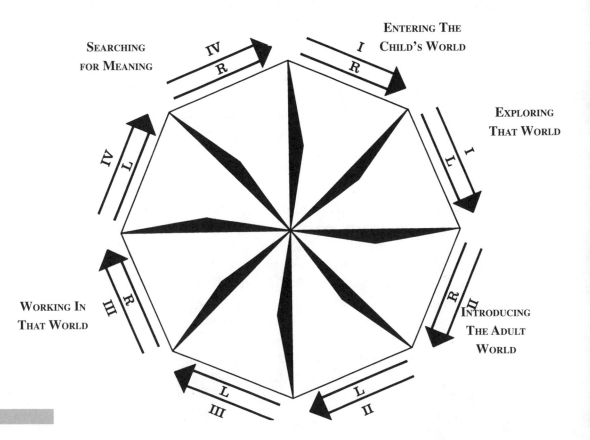

The pinwheel pointed to a sequence, giving structure to their team planning sessions.

CULTURE: PAST, PRESENT, AND FUTURE

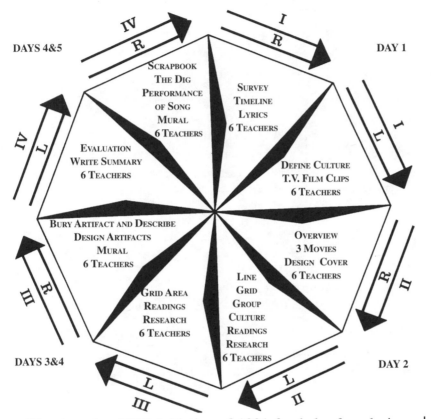

The America 2000 initiative of 1991 funded a few design teams to hone their philosophies, their experiences, their hopes, their dreams to create new architectures for schools of the future.

One such design team entered the national competition for funding with the concept of curriculum as life experiences centered around community home bases. A home base could well be a shopping mall where students come and go with their experiences orchestrated and monitored by a small group of teachers. These teachers could be business professionals or other community workers as well as certified educators. This design team, calling themselves "St. Louis Metro 2000," is beginning an implementation phase funded through a cooperative of local sources. The effort goes under the logo, "It takes a village to raise a child."

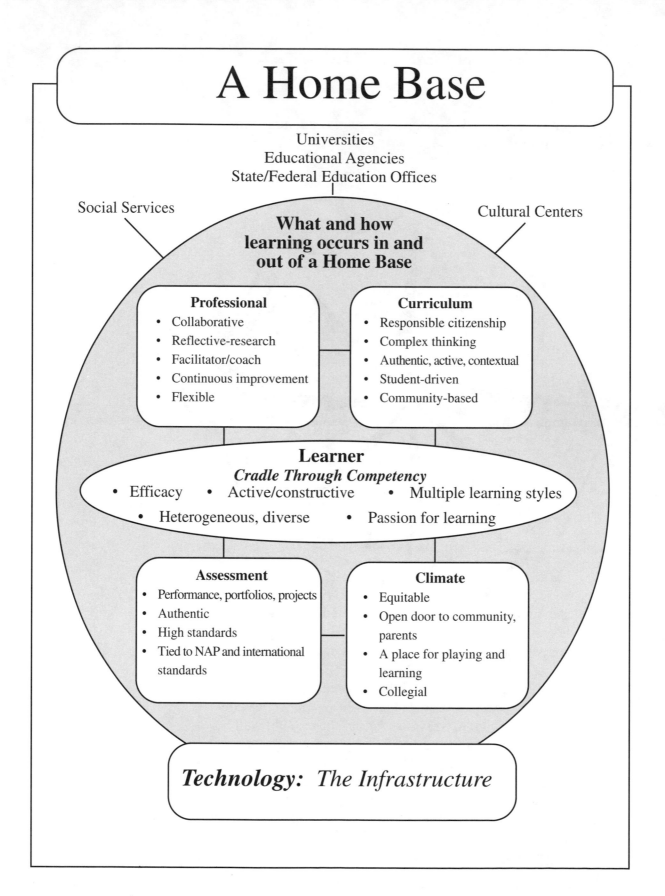

A Home Base

Universities
Educational Agencies
State/Federal Education Offices

Social Services

Cultural Centers

What and how learning occurs in and out of a Home Base

Professional
- Collaborative
- Reflective-research
- Facilitator/coach
- Continuous improvement
- Flexible

Curriculum
- Responsible citizenship
- Complex thinking
- Authentic, active, contextual
- Student-driven
- Community-based

Learner
Cradle Through Competency
- Efficacy
- Active/constructive
- Multiple learning styles
- Heterogeneous, diverse
- Passion for learning

Assessment
- Performance, portfolios, projects
- Authentic
- High standards
- Tied to NAP and international standards

Climate
- Equitable
- Open door to community, parents
- A place for playing and learning
- Collegial

Technology: *The Infrastructure*

In Real Time

My hands were muffled in oversized gloves
    wired to machines I knew not of.
My head was encased in a helmet-like device
    with other-world goggles.
My breath came in ragged gulps
    as the event approached.

I was in a room, a real room. As I turned my head left, my eyes landscaped the perimeter of the room. Turning right, I tracked back along my visual field past my initial starting point, on even further right around the room until the panorama was complete. I reached out and picked up a vase. One hand held the sculpted vase as the other delicately picked out a single red rose.

I was there. But not there,

    "All ponies, all ponies, open order NOW!
      Prepare for possible contact."
    "Sierra six-five, this is Mike niner-niner.
     Over."
    "One, one, break off and check the site for
     survivors. . . break . . . break. One-three.
    What you got back there? Somebody on
     our six? . . . Gander, Gander. You get the
     boggy on the right. I'll take the left."

I was there. But not there.

I was drained as I climbed down from the flight simulator.

Virtual Reality…a marvel of the technological wizards. We can now experience dogfights, be in a room where we are not. See vistas at arm's length.

Virtual reality, a newcomer to our high technology world, is a concept that opens up the possibility that we do not have to be somewhere to experience it. With human friendly technology and human literate programs based on artificial intelligence, life ventures can be experienced through simulation. Learning and life experiences are inextricably bound. That's the way life is. We experience. We participate. We respond viscerally, and we are never quite the same again. That's learning. Life and learning.

Somehow schools have placed themselves square in the middle between life and learning. School is always ABOUT something. Never something itself. We read about history. We never live history. We talk about explorers, we don't explore. We study about architecture and Doric columns, we don't build things. We practice on work sheets about math facts; we don't probe the dimensions of life space.

Somehow in the interest of efficiency and managing large numbers of children, we forgot that living is learning. And education should be about learning and living. The real thing. Not a child's take-an-ole-'tater and wait version of Sunday dinner, but the whole feast itself. School should be real. Learning at school could be experiencing and processing in real time, a virtual reality.

Chapter Five

Pitfalls

ot all curriculum architecture is inherently good. There are pitfalls; situations in which design issues were determined in an inappropriate decision-making process.

A visual representation of this problem includes two versions of a pyramid. Throughout the years, the education pyramid, a top-down model, has negatively affected curricular decisions.The curriculum design of the school has been driven by the organizational factors of how the school is arranged, where teachers are placed, and where students go. It should be the design of the curriculum that determines these decisions. The decision-making structure would then be an *inverted* pyramid. How the school is staffed should depend on the architecture of the curriculum the teachers have designed. For example, Cross Keys staff should be organized around how to best implement the pinwheels; whereas, Brown Barge's staffing structure should be determined by how to best implement their streams and tiers.

An inverted decision-making pyramid is needed in the budget arena. Usually, the budget drives the program instead of the program driving the budget. Zero-based budgeting would have school leaders requesting funds based on their program intents. Although they may not secure the amount requested, they could be given a percentage which still reflects their curriculum planning. All too often, however, a budget is divided into equal parts with no opportunity to reflect unique architectural design.

Programmatic decisions also are made inappropriately when the concept of curriculum architecture is not understood. In one school flush with Carl Perkins money newly targeted in a very narrow program field, extensive equipment was purchased to augment a ninth grade program for a special needs population: robotics, graphics and cad cam appeared almost instantly. In preparation for the new program, ninth graders were distributed into five-member teacher teams with commonly shared students, assigned randomly. All of these decisions were consistent with current recommendations of restructuring.

The equipment worked. But, there was no curriculum. There was no master plan for student access. The result was an expensive lesson. A pyramidal disaster.

Another pitfall occurs when planners are confused about the essential nature of curriculum.

A side trip. Mom and Dad moved to West Texas leaving longtime friends in Oklahoma. An annual trek to their origin occurred every year. For over fifteen years, half of the five hundred mile journey was devoted to the issue of what is the "best" route to get there. Mom said the best route was through Synder via Big Spring. Dad claimed vehemently that Farm Road #2906 was "best." Then both disputants scrutinized the most recent state map. Mileage was recounted. Discrepancies of even five miles or less were resolved. Despite all of this attention, time and intensity, the issue eluded resolution.

It was only when a backseat rider ignored the map and observed the landscape rolling by the side window that the issue became clear. The reason why Mom's route was better was that the territory included Synder's restaurant, a true chicken fried steak palace that did Texas proud. Dad's route was best because the territory he faced as a driver was void of the interstate's heavily loaded semi's. The two navigators could not agree because they persisted in looking at the map, not the territory.

A map is a symbol, some abstraction of something real. As abstractions, or symbol systems, maps are very useful. But people forget that the map is just a symbol, not to be confused with reality itself. A map may be an extraordinarily accurate abstraction; yet, still symbolic, not the real thing, not authentic, not the territory itself.

Semanticists have formed this phenomenon of language and

its symbol system into a rule for high quality communications: The map is not the territory. Breaking this rule causes problems.

The American public is prone to anger to the point of vigilantism if a protestor burns an American Flag. Time after time, bills have been brought before Congress to make such a transgression a felony. So far, calmer heads have voted them down. It is not that people who resist becoming inflamed by such irreverent actions as flag burning are less patriotic or somehow are more wimp-like when compared to their fervored fellow citizens. It is just that some of the population knows not to confuse the flag, a symbol of the country, with the country itself. Those who seek to punish protestors' flag-burning actions have confused the map and the territory, misguidedly elevating the flag, a piece of material with red and white stripes and blue stars, to be a country itself. A flag is a flag. A country is a country. Patriotism is a feeling that finds expression in reverence for a country's flag.

To enlighten dialogue in situations where maps and territories have been confused, participants must discard the map and return to the territory itself as the point of discussion.

When issues of curriculum surface, often disputes arise because those who construct curriculum have broken "the map is not the territory" rule. School is a map that serves to simulate life for students. School is artificial in that it was constructed and continues to act in place of real life experiences. Perhaps the original idea of education was for students to retreat to an "ivory tower" existence with a learned mentor and guide to reflect on the meaning of life. Somehow translated through the ages we have arrived at the 20th century school which is a building with teachers, periods, content, activities, goals, objectives and all the other accoutrements that have come to stand for life.

We are far removed from the tribal way of education that immerses a young brave in actual hunts for food and in governance meetings of the tribe. When we develop curriculum, or make our plans of access to learning for students, we must re-

> We must remember that school is one mass simulation and is not real life.

member that school is one mass simulation and is not real life. Therefore, we need not hang on to rituals devised in the name of simulation such as grades to stand for effort, textbooks to stand for knowledge, tests as proof of learning. These elements are not to be preserved as inherently worthy. They are just maps constructed by humans somewhere, sometime, not an actual territory. They are an elaborate symbol system created for a large youth population who are more efficiently sheltered in an artificial atmosphere rather than sent to participate in daily life in a real world. The curriculum is no more real than the bathosphere designed to simulate earth's ecosystems in the Arizona flatlands.

> **As our curriculum maps have endured through generations, they have fallen behind in the degree to which they accurately reflect reality.**

Further, as our curriculum maps have endured through generations, they have fallen behind in the degree to which they accurately reflect reality. Learning to write solely with a pencil does not reflect 1990s authors. Ciphering without a calculator is a poor representation of how the real world enumerates. When professionals find themselves in dispute over curricular issues such as, "Should Algebra start in the eighth grade?" we must go to the real issue, discarding the map of Algebra and return to the territory, which is how to introduce students to the world of symbol systems.

As we deal with creating a curriculum architecture, the prime goal is to stay as close to life itself, discarding as many intervening maps as possible. The architecture should accommodate an authentic curriculum, or plan of student access to life and learning opportunities. We may not be able to expose all students to kayaking up the Amazon, but neither must we fool ourselves into believing that reading about such an experience is an indispensable piece of curriculum that cannot be reconsidered. All curriculum, as maps, not territories, should be under constant scrutiny for efficacy in facilitating a learning process for students. Curriculum that maintains its place through tradition while losing any relationship to reality should be retired.

Curriculum development should be an attempt to orchestrate actual life experiences; second best is to make a good map. The best map is the one that is most congruent with the territory; therefore, the curriculum plan should promote integration because life is integrated.

It is in this concept of map and territories that the rationale for an integrated curriculum takes form. The curriculum should be built around concepts that intersect students' authentic concerns with society's authentic issues (Beane, 1993). Further, the prime value is that school not be a simulation any more than it has to be. Kids' experiences in school should be authentic, should be as much "territory" as they can be and as little "map" as possible.

Unfortunately, most schools are first organized in some fashion long before the curriculum surfaces as an issue. Most reform efforts have been beached on the shoals of their own creation. The very word "restructure" connotes a rearrangement of existing parts. The middle school movement is a prime example of improvement efforts stalled because the main issues revolve around how the school should be arranged. In teams? With certain grades? With advisory? Block scheduling? These elements are all maps, not territories. None of these elements will affect achievement or impact student learning unless the curriculum itself has been the organizing principle—unless the curricular architecture is designed first.

Another pitfall is that curriculum developers "just don't get it." Curriculum architecture must be begun by reaching an understanding of its essential nature. Everything has such an essential nature. This essential nature is usually part of common thought. Thinking gets fuzzy when we miss the essential nature of something.

In *Huck Finn*, Huck and his raft partner, Jim, had many languid days upon the Mississippi to contemplate the essential nature of things. Scarcely a concept escaped their notice. One such discussion centered around, "Why French men don't speak English?"

> Curriculum development should be an attempt to orchestrate actual life experiences; second best is to make a good map.

Why, Huck, doan' de French people talk de same way we does?

No, Jim; you couldn't understand a word they said—not a single word.

Well, now, I be ding-busted! How do dat come?

I don't know; but it's so. I got some of their jabber out of a book. S'pose a man was to come to you and say Polly-voo-franzy—what would you think?

I wouldn't think nuffn; I'd take en bust him over de head —dat is, if he warn't white. . . .

Shucks, it ain't calling you anything. It's only saying, do you know how to talk French?

Well, den, why couldn't he say it?

Why, he is a-saying it. That's a Frenchman's way of saying it.

Well, it's a blame ridicklous way, en I doan' want to hear no mo' 'bout it. Dey ain' no sense in it.

Looky here, Jim; does a cat talk like we do?

No, a cat don't.

Well does a cow?

No, a cow don't, nuther.

Does a cat talk like a cow, or a cow talk like a cat?

No, dey don't.

It's natural and right for 'em to talk different from each other, ain't it?

Course.

And ain't it natural and right for a cat and a cow to talk different from us?

Why, mos' sholy it is.

Well, then, why ain't it natural and right for a Frenchman to talk different from us? You answer me that.

Is a cat a man, Huck?

No.

Well, den, dey ain't no sense in a cat talkin' like a man. Is a cow a man? —er is a cow a cat?

No, she ain't either of them.

Well, den, she ain't got no business to talk like either one er the yuther of 'em. Is a Frenchman a man?

Yes.

Well, den! Dad blame it, why doan' he talk like a man? You answer me dat!

Finally, the two conversants got down to the essential nature of it.

Even Professor Henry Higgins had a moment when the essential nature of it caught his imagination and he shouted out in frustration, "Why can't a woman be more like a man?" And then a whole 'nother story fell out of that.

A monograph? It has an essential nature commonly understood. One would not expect a plot right here in the middle of Chapter 5 nor would a debate over its use of characterization ever get started. Because it's not the nature of it.

Curriculum architecture thus begins by replacing a faulty, although commonly held, conception of the very nature of it.

Educators have been taught that curriculum is the same as what the teacher does. What the teacher does one year is inextricably linked to what the teacher will do next year. And, for that matter, what the teacher did the year before. In this fashion, education becomes one long string of interlocking links becoming longer and longer, thicker and thicker as a child moves through the curriculum, or, what the teacher directs. We've been taught that curriculum is like salt water taffy that starts as a plop of glop. Then, as it is wound around two sets of hands some distance apart, it becomes longer and longer, thinner and thinner. A "taffy pull" it's called. So even though its form may have changed from a single plop to multiple sumptuous sweet morsels, its essential nature has not changed.

Teachers have determined what place their curriculum has in relationship to all the other links, whether their decision for their plan came to them through osmosis, imitation, or studied thought. Hardly from infamous articulation meetings.

Many teachers think the curriculum is a chain of links. Every year in school is seen as irreplaceable and forms a vital link in constructing a complete chain. A student is missing valuable, irreplaceable experiences if last night's homework were not done. All missing assignments must be made up. A student with "A's" on tests and "Incompletes" on all other work cannot possibly be promoted to the next "link." A student whose chain is shorter than everyone else's is retained.

This conception of the curriculum as links in a chain falters when compared to reality. A forty-year old truly never would miss the curriculum from December, 1964 to February, 1965 when he had mononucleosis. A night's worth or even six nights of homework missed in math would not stunt the development of a young astronaut-to-be. A retainee who stayed in eighth grade two years would never lengthen his chain with surety. So, the curriculum as a chain just doesn't suit its essential nature. The chain is a neat, compact, rational idea; just not very accurate about the very nature of curriculum.

But upon the scene comes a technology that can replace this illogical perception of the very nature of curriculum. The essential nature of curriculum is not a linked chain. Instead, it is portraits of pixels. Pixels are those minute electronic dots or pixs that when bunched together in certain patterns form an image. Beaming pixels electronically is how a picture comes to be on a television screen. Sending pixels optically through telephone cables produces "faxes." One purchases a computer printer partly by using a criterion of the number of pixels per inch. In pixel talk, more is better. High resolution TV has gobs of pixels. A meager Apple IIe screen is woefully pixel short when compared to a colorrama Macintosh one.

Curriculum is a plan of access for students to create whole images of life. Throughout students' lifetimes, they add pixels of understanding to their life portraits. Those who add lots of pixels have rich and enduring, while ever-changing, sets of images. Others' stock of images may be of lesser quality because, in sum, their experiences which generated pixels did not produce a critical enough mass to form crystal clear images. These students suffer from an impoverished curriculum.

Pixels about life are not produced only in a school setting. A forty-year old who missed curriculum from December, 1964 to February, 1965, yet still functions, illustrates how those few missing pixels did not lessen the quality of the images he carries through life.

Curriculum is a plan to accumulate pixels; to make wondrous pictures. The plan is not forging links in an iron chain. That is not its essential nature.

We must be willing to give up the notion that:

- everyone has to learn the same thing from a given experience

- there is a right or wrong answer. The important activity is the constructing of meaning—not judging

- there is an inherent order—sequence is important

- to study the whole, the parts must be known

- there is one source of information—an authority

- the main input device is reading

- everything that is done must be recorded and evaluated.

- the purpose of education is to acquire knowledge.

Curriculum architecture, then, should emerge from creative and informed thinking that recognizes the purpose of education is to construct meaning. The curriculum is forged anew rather than already existing as a product of old notions, bad metaphors, troublesome semantic snarls, and misidentification of its very essence. Eliminating these thinking errors, educators can be free to create.

purpose for advisement is to develop a relationship with each child, it makes perfect sense that advisement occurs best when an advisor and an advisee meet alone.

We can avoid a teapot caper. An advisement program can be totally individual. That means we can avoid food drives, candy sales, punching green tickets, forming circles, electing officers, raffling cold turkeys and other things advisors are heir to.

What we do is find common ground with a student and have dialogues. Long talks. Short talks. Some paper. Some tasks. All activity is initiated simply to allow a forum for a relationship to develop, to flourish. Perhaps this natural logic: *if you want to build a relationship, go find the person and start one* is too straightforward. Surely it can't be that way, but it is so.

Chapter Six

Living in the Question

The decade of the 90s is also the decade of the 90th anniversary of the first airplane flight of Orville and Wilbur Wright at Kitty Hawk. As the century mark approaches so will a major centennial in the history of flight. From an inaugural flight of 120', barely the wing span of current domestic airliners, to the era of Top Guns, laser-guided bombing runs, and the prospect of renting rooms on the Soviet Space Station. From a twelve second flight to a legion of Century 21 agents. Almost one hundred years of progress.

Orville and Wilbur little could have imagined the future that flight was to have; yet, this unforeseeable future must have been what moved them to take the risks associated with that first flight. We now know, however, that the Wright Brothers made a strategic mistake that was destined to be repeated over and over for the full 90 years. Although the many components of that first aircraft were carefully designed and tested, these early day pilots ran out of time. When General Octave Chanute urged that the fixed wing design be changed to a flexible wing design, the brothers W. flew their first flight with their tested fixed wing. When the flight was successful, planes have had fixed wings from that day throughout nine decades. The fixed wing is so much a part of the "architecture" of an airplane that we could imagine our being distraught if, in the middle of our flight from LAX. to O'Hare, we looked out the window and the wing moved.

In the early 90s we now know that designing the airplane with a fixed wing causes multiple problems that current day travelers just assume are part of the experience of flying. Turbulence, wind shears, stalls, and gas guzzling stem from the fixed wing design. So do almost all small craft fatalities and 25% of major air disasters. For the Wright Brothers' running out of testing time, we have had 90 years of air sickness. No one questioned the fixed wing decision. It became unthinkable that an airplane with loosy-goosy wings could fly.

It is a characteristic of human behavior that when a workable solution is found, the opportunity to revisit that decision diminishes. Frankly, it fades to zero. Throughout 32,850 days of flying since then, no one asked. To prevent such a mistake as we plan for unforeseeable futures, we must continue to live in the question. It is difficult for human beings to force themselves to re-ask questions and revisit solutions that have been successful. The original question becomes outside our perceptual field. In the final decade of the twentieth century, there will be aircraft with flexible wings. Even highly trained pilots may find their skills obsolete. Soon they will be physiologically incapable of flying a plane as we now know the act of "flying" to be. There may be a cyborg that will take a pilot's place to maneuver flexible wings. What an unforeseeable future that will be!

We can look to children's ancient play of skating for insight into other solutions unexamined. Skates, as most generations have known them, were fitted to the shoe with clamps tightened by a skate key. To keep the whereabouts of the key known, it was common to wear it on a string around the neck. Youngsters learned to balance themselves atop the four wheels underneath each foot. Somewhere in history those wheels were made of wood, but the wheels changed composition as newer, stronger materials were developed. But today, one does not buy skates. "Blades" is the department where these one-time-toys-now-turned-athletic-equipment can be found. Not only is the signature of the blades neon, but also the wheels are not Noah's Ark two-by-two but in-a- line. In-line skates were possible long before now. No one ever thought of them. No one questioned the four wheel design for all these many years. Yet, blades allow fluidity of movement akin to skating on ice. Now that the question, "What should skates be like?" has been asked again, we wonder why we never asked it long before.

It is true that design, or form, is inextricably tied to function. If blades, or skates-in-a-line, restricted locomotion, they would not replace the four wheelers. If the over-the-tip ski jump form resulted in more crash landings, the new style would never be designed. If airplanes with flexible wings caused more accidents, they would never make it off the production line. If bicycles by form refused to move, they would never be produced.

If school never educated anyone, it would not look like it does today. Forms that are successful for their time and in their generation die very hard. It could be said that we in schools are victims of our past success. It could be said that since schools don't "live in the question," they are trapped in their own image.

Of course, school must be a place. Or must it? Of course, teachers must "teach." Or must they? It is only when we continue to live in the question as part of our daily behavior that we become the flexible problem solvers our new century demands of us as educators. Further, teaching our students to live in the question will also free them to become problem solvers and, therefore, resilient citizens for tomorrow. In schools there just are certain questions that educators must always "live in." "What should schools be like?" And, "How do people learn?"

This rule of living in the question provides a rationale for the notion that curriculum should have an architecture that is designed and redesigned. The construction of a curricular architecture demands that we examine old decisions and rethink our metaphors routinely.

Our willingness to live in the question also solves another problem. Doctor, lawyer, merchant, chief—rich man, poor man, beggar man, thief. What if, we add the word "teacher." Just as surely as "doctor" conjures up a white-coated middle aged male with stethoscope, so does "teacher" reflect just as precise an image. Teachers are earnest. They always stand up. They have a book from which to teach. What they say goes. They decide what the group should do. To prevent a child from growing up in less than favorable ways, the teacher is to report to the parent

Of course, school must be a place. Or must it? Of course, teachers must "teach." Or must they?

65

progress, or the lack thereof, along with personality defects. Teachers are the final authority for what is true. Teachers must know what they teach. To whom they teach it is of much less importance.

This image of ourselves is what allows us to participate on textbook selection committees without questioning whether or not we need textbooks. This image of ourselves is what allows us to construct elaborate rule systems for controlling children without asking whether rule-making frees learners to learn. This image of ourselves is what allows us to limit all learners to what we know rather than ask the question, "What is there out there to learn?" Under the guise of making lesson plans, which is part of our image, we make all the decisions rather than live in the question, "What decisions do learners need to make?" Teaming as a solution occurs only if we live in the question, "What do students need for resources?"

Our image of ourselves is so strong that, in some, it becomes interwoven into the personality. Teaming then becomes a force destructive to our very being. Why is change hard? Because who we are is caught up in what we do. And what we do takes the place of what the question is. We have been destined to repeat these mistakes for over five hundred years since school was formalized. It is time to exercise our ability to live in the question.

Why is change hard? Because who we are is caught up in what we do. And what we do takes the place of what the question is.

In the mid 90s, the curve of reform that started in the early 80s with "the rising tide of mediocrity" has turned into statewide reformations centered on the notion that content must be reconsidered. The newest wave of reform has us gather together in one shining palace the collective wisdom of our age. And, in a series of intense subject matter conversations, the content that shall be the baseline for future reform is carved out. As long as high level forums start at the premise that education must decide what content everyone should know, the best curricular thought of our time will not be living in the question. Instead, by an extension of rational thought, these thinkers will promote the notion that consensus on outcomes can next be followed by a consensus on content standards only then to be followed by consensus on performance and further will become linked to school-to-work connections. This thinking does not allow for unforeseeable futures. Disappointment, if not national dishonor, may come when students who have been left out of this neat framework make their presence known in classrooms all over the country designed in such fashion. Instead of this scenario, professionals at work with children should continue to design a curricular architecture. Arguments should be over what design best encourages learning, not which content best serves as a framework for an entire academic field. Focusing on learning forces one to live in the question. Standards, reforms, outcomes and all the other reform strategies can't work if the design, or plan of access, is not also addressed.

To the pain of individuals who see their personalities "assaulted" by new solutions to the question, "What is a teacher?" we must now add the pain of highly influential educational organizations such as state departments with collaboration from their top-ranked consultants. Even if we give the "standard bearers" the benefit of acknowledging ahead of the conclusion of their work that they indeed can reach consensus on what content should be taught, we would still be left with the question, "How are students going to learn it?" It isn't the setting of standards that is difficult. The difficult part is how do we engage youngsters in learning that content when, in the first row alone, there is one child who is a victim of child abuse, one who is homeless, one who has attention deficit disorder, one whose family is unstable, one whose single mother is out of work, and one who lives just down the street from a crack house. And that's only the front row. Take this one row of six and multiply it by five more rows. Now, that is the magnitude of the question. It is not a matter of content. It is a matter of establishing relationships with students and establishing connections that make sense to those who inhabit the desks. Educators who so willingly, in fact gratefully, take shelter in the standards setting movement someday will find their own pain caused by not living in the question. They have a fixed wing.

Standards based on content do not allow for unforeseeable futures. What is a widely accepted standard of content today can be rendered obsolete when, seemingly overnight, a discovery, a

> We have to forego content with which we are comfortable in favor of a willingness to live in the ambiguity of designing plans that allow students to learn.

revolutionary notion, or a new paradigm comes forth on the five o'clock news. We must not confuse curriculum with content standards. We must have a plan of access to world class standards, not just set them. This plan of access for students is the curriculum.

Educational leaders must shed the comfort of wrestling intellectually with peers while setting content standards. Those leaders appointed to set the standards surely will complete their task. The content that survives the heat of discourse will emerge as national content standards. But it is the plan that is key; not the standards. To shift our focus from setting content standards to the curriculum itself will be painful, because we have to forego content with which we are comfortable and discussions that are stimulating in favor of a willingness to live in the ambiguity of designing plans that allow students to learn. For example, it is much easier, more comfortable, to decide what history is important than it is to tackle such an issue as the iron chain that links success in school with high socioeconomic level. It is not that we don't know what history is important; we do. After rubbing noses for a bit, we could even reach consensus. But, we don't know how to make poor kids successful at learning history. We will have to wrestle painfully with this "politically incorrect" issue if we design a curriculum architecture, or a plan of access. And no consensus on content "standards" is going to illuminate this issue, but it will avoid the pain.

Further, when educators publish a final list of content standards, they probably envision an interlocking system of standards webbing the whole country together, underpinned by the outcome statements that can then be turned into a statewide accountability system. From the standards, local educators can carve up the content into appropriate grade levels with scope and multicolored sequence charts. Classroom teachers at each grade will then take their chunk of the content and spread it out across a year of instruction in one period per day segments. The package will be neat, sequential, and inimitably explainable. Just such a system, derived from logic, changed our multiple, poorly maintained highways into the amazing interstate roadways crisscrossing the nation today. Sometimes, those logical designs are very effective.

But in other cases, a logic is not enough. What worked with highways won't work with curriculum. Building such a reductionist framework system as national content standards is like building super highways that go nowhere. It has no relationship to helping students learn. The question is not, "Where should we go?" The question is, "How are we going to get kids there?"

The same conundrum will soon emerge around technology. The history of the world embellished with photographs, film clips, sound, and authentic color on a CD ROM for the fair market price of three hundred dollars is already at the fingertips of every child. But, set a student (like one of those in the front row) in front of an inexpensive computer with a CD ROM and dead silence might ensue. The question is what is the student going to do with it? Even technology with all of its promise cannot be harnessed as an educational work horse without a curricular design.

Another example of the pain of living in the question is the history of desegregation in the United States. The question is, "How can we prevent some students from having all the education while others have little?" For the modern century, schools were unwilling to live in that question, blending themselves into the wallpaper of foundation formulas that continued to give more to those who had a property tax base while those without a viable property tax base received little. Current reforms in school financing are beginning to live in the question. Education served up according to where students live is beginning to end. But, it is notable that this change was not led by educators. It had to be forced by lawyers and courts. Local educators who noticed the inequality but did nothing about it did not want to bear the pain of the question.

Living in the question requires moral courage.

Living in the question requires moral courage. Changemakers who live in the question and who lead groups into considering the question must defend themselves from those who refuse to leave their own comfort zone. Changemakers experience pain.

School organizations will cause pain when they force consideration of the question through leaders who have moral courage. Living in the question requires a higher level of dialogue among colleagues. Lest some be seen as inadequate, they go for the jugular of those who are willing to live in those hard to ask and even harder to answer questions.

We must take on ourselves the pain of living in the question to absolve the pain of our children who are not succeeding with our old solutions. It is not that schools need to have all the answers, but that the right questions are being asked.

Sometimes decisions are hard, and the changes that need to be made are neither comfortable nor convenient. These changes may feel awkward or require an enormous amount of effort to counteract the inertia of past decisions. Those who participate in making difficult decisions frequently face the possibility that they will be isolated and ostracized by their colleagues for making needed but not popular decisions. Some are able to lead the school in making substantive changes for students despite the pain. Character, strength, talent, expertise, and vision will be needed to lead others to live in the question. To find new and different perspectives, to inform the problems in schools, we must ask questions which are hard to ask. It is in the asking that change will occur. We must learn how to ask questions by living in them.

Schools like Cross Keys Middle School or Brown-Barge Middle School that pioneered transformation had one quality in common. They were committed to something they did not know how to do. To be successful, other schools just beginning the change also must be willing to commit themselves to something they don't know how to do. From those who have emerged as exemplary middle schools, can come the identification of those issues that will prove to be the defining line. These schools cannot give solutions to questions, for solutions must grow from the setting in which the questions were asked. But those who go before can define those backbreaking issues that, if left unconquered, prohibit transformation.

To find new and different perspectives, to inform the problems in schools, we must ask hard questions.

Issues to be conquered

Each issue comes laden with vested constituencies, rich and noble histories, and the power of previous persuasion. Yet, these issues must be conquered for a true middle school to emerge.

1. Tracking. The process of sorting students along a continuum from low ability to high ability seems to be creditable because it masquerades as being grounded in rational thought. Bright students can go faster and cover more. Slower students can cover less and need more time, the logic goes. Therefore, we should group like with like. Such a happening is common in nature. "Birds of a feather flock together," so goes the saying. Yet, extensive research has proven otherwise. Not only social gains but also academic gains are made from eliminating academic groups based on presumed ability. The tracking issue will shake transforming middle schools down to their very foundations with colleagues aligned against colleagues. Yet, tracking must be removed in middle schools to unencumber the learning process.

2. Level of teaming. It takes only a keyboard command to schedule teachers and students in teams. This organizational technique enables teachers to share students in common and is so beneficial that teachers are prone to stop the development of their team process at the early entry point. To reach the outer limits of teaming where content lines dissolve in favor of integrated learning activities is a real struggle. When teaming loses its "convenience" label and begins to require personal change for teachers, this defining issue proves resistant to evolution.

3. Algebra. Let's start the outline of this backbreaker by first putting algebra in its proper context. Algebra is but a fly speck on the butcher paper of the history of mankind. Algebra is used as a back breaker in another sense also. It is a course that forever divides Americans into another kind of haves and have nots. The haves can pass algebra. The have nots must forever live in infamy. Algebra is the tollgate to higher education as if America's higher institutions do not have room for everybody. Why algebra is the gatekeeper is a mystery. They might as well let in blondes and exclude all red-

> Algebra is a course that forever divides Americans into another kind of haves and have nots.

heads. Further, algebra in middle school allows high school mathematics teachers to teach their favorite subjects, most commonly the higher end of a sequence of algebra, geometry, trigonometry, and calculus. Even as math educators begin to swing toward problem-solving content rather than a prerequisite sequence of course offerings, algebra remains a defining issue at middle school. To balance the positions of algebra as a must and algebra as expendable, the architecture used must be designed to accommodate both without tracking. Seeing algebra as a "course" will break the back of any reform movement.

4. Equity. There is some immutable force at work in schools that continually undermines efforts to ensure equity for every child. No sooner is one puff of the pigs equity house deflected than another puff from an entirely different direction blows the house down. The origins of inequity range all the way from state mandated standards to decisions that look oh so simple, like what electives should be offered? A state mandated and funded program for the gifted, in and of itself, need not be counter to equity, but it becomes so when the only measures the state sanctions to identify gifted students are academic test scores. These may not be equitable across cultures and learning styles. Some schools conserve manpower by allowing student choices of music and foreign language to compete with art or technology. It is a single step from that thinking to thinking also that the valued choices are orchestra and band. It doesn't really matter what the other choices are, too many schools believe. Changing this inequity is a backbreaker.

5. Retention. Again, unquestionable research that proves the futility of the practice of retention is often disregarded. Those who promote retention do so with a ferocity withering in its firepower. It is difficult to refute, even with statistics, the construct of failure. Starting with, "Its good for you," all the way to "You deserve it," the morality enfolding retention makes it almost unassailable. Yet, based on lifelong damage to students caused by retention, seeking its demise should become a moral crusade.

6. Giving up something. There is the proverbial five pound bag. No amount of shoving can exceed the weight limit; therefore, schools must give up the notion of covering content as the purpose of education. Each professional must live in the question, "What is essential to know?" and have the presence of mind to separate the answer to that question from the answer to this question, "What do I like to teach?" Teachers keep their favorite curriculum that is as comfortable as their mother's lap. Most of these units will have to be eliminated to make room for integrated units constructed around essential concepts. The act of tucking these treasures away in the attic of our memory is painful.

7. Standardized test scores. If learning grows dendrites and if standardized testing distributes along a continuum those who have them from those who don't, then test scores should rise even if we don't cover any preferred content. The best hope of increasing achievement for our students lies in the amount and the degree of engagement in learning that we can orchestrate. Middle schoolers who are active in learning will outperform middle schoolers who are passive in the schooling process. The evidence to support this position is now available from the pioneering schools.

8. Shoe on the other foot. It is now time that the burden of proof relative to the efficacy of middle school tenants must shift from those proponents now armed with evidence and research to those defenders of current practice who are armed only with custom and history. The question must shift from, "Why?" to "Why not?" By demanding professional rigor from those who would undermine the middle school transformation process, initiators can shed their role as defenders.

9. Who's your audience? The right answer to questions rightly asked is hard to come by because the answer differs according to the audience to whom the answerer plays. Some educators play to teachers. Any solution that pleases teachers is considered to be a good solution. Other educators play to a parent audience. Any solution that keeps parents content is an accept-

> The best hope of increasing achievement for our students lies in the amount and the degree of engagement in learning that we can orchestrate.

able solution. Still others identify audiences based upon the degree of fear generated. We must bring to consciousness our own audience that forever sits on our shoulder ready to condemn what we do or praise what it craves. With courage, we can overcome our own nemesis. The only acceptable criteria to judge answers are those answers that result in good for children.

> Accomplishing the vision of middle school requires cultural change as well as organizational change.

10. Culture change. The seminal work, *Turning Points* (1989) outlines the change agenda—teams, advisory, block scheduling. But what it doesn't tell us is that accomplishing the vision of middle school requires cultural change. The results are still out as to whether organizational cultures can be changed. But, at least, we should not misconstrue the field upon which the battle will be fought. We must know that living in the question and being committed to doing something we do not know how to do are, in and of themselves, antithetical to some certain common school cultures. Those that prize routine, those that rest on past achievement, those that intend to hold out until the energetic have exhausted themselves pinned down on the cultural beachhead will be forever crouched behind a hard wall that is difficult, if not impossible, to break through. Hard cultures are backbreakers.

Much current writing about middle school transformation has us believe that the issues schools must resolve are scheduling, advisory, teaming, and other such topics. These are not the backbreakers. But, mistakenly focusing on these topics can delay by years the recognition and resolution of the true issues of middle school change.

TRUTHS AND FALSEHOODS

The first headline news story is that much of what our experts have been telling us about change is true. It is true that meaningful change is possible. It is true that change is painful but promising. It is true that the job is never finished because change is continuous, but the readily visible hallmarks along the way give a sense of accomplishment. It is true that the leadership must lead with vision. It is true that leaders can change an organization's culture, but this change does not result in a change of peoples' personalities but can set the tone of the work environment.

Now. Five truths is pretty good, but what is false is extraordinary. A falsehood—You don't have to have widespread involvement in determining change directions. Common advice is to coalesce diverse opinions and let the group as a whole figure out where to go. Frankly, you know, the Big Bang theory of the beginning of our solar system posits that mass hung around until it formed into this big ball and then BANG—out came the planets and created a Universe. But look how long that creation took. We don't have that kind of time. Instead, the change direction must be definitive with implementation issues open for discussion. As world class weight lifters know, this is the "clean and jerk" method of change.

Another falsehood. Teachers always know best. Well, much of the time they do, but those closest to the situation have the least opportunity to gain a degree of perspective. Teachers' daily attention is riveted to the task at hand and broad perspective is not a characteristic easily attained in a teacher's environment. The broad perspective and change direction must be set with teacher consensus, but not necessarily teacher initiation.

The best falsehood is this last one. This one is a Bigggeeeeeeeeeeeee. It is not true that when a school adopts an integrated curricular change that test scores may decline and require us to defend that change. Achievement increases when you throw out all the units you spent the last ten years designing with objectives cross referenced to the test objectives. Just think all those years we thought we were preparing students academically for the test, and we weren't. If we had spent an equal amount of energy in the direction of integration, thematic approaches, our achievement performance probably would not have been in trouble in the first place.

LEADING WITH THE BEST

Pink flamingos on the front lawn—that's one thing that Americans do better than anyone else in the world, according to *Courvoisier's Book of the Best*. And eating hamburgers. Americans are ***the very best*** at the rate of two billion a day. Among the things that *Couvoisier's* didn't list is leadership models. Americans are the very best at creating leadership structures that suit the enterprise.

There's the military model. It is efficient and orderly. It may win wars, but it's not good for creative environments.

Then there's the town meeting variety. Democratic. Good for involvement, but not very time conserving. How about a representative model like republics have? Good for dialogue, but short on action.

Just to name a few.

So, Americans create many leadership configurations. But, schools, contrary to truly exemplary enterprises, aren't too good at using the appropriate leadership model to suit the mission at hand.

Schools basically operate with one of three models. The principal runs the show, the teachers run the show, or standing committees abide and stagnate like pond scum.

When it comes to the need for restructuring, this situation just will not do. Restructuring calls for many decisions to be made. Most schools do not have processes designed to make them. Schools first have to design the ways decisions are going to be made before effective decision-making can occur.

Chapter Seven

Getting Started

ssume you have just been made Master-of-Change in your district. And you have just been dunked in a tepid bath of despair after reading this month's issue of *Middle School Journal, Educational Leadership,* or *Kappan.* You look around and feel singularly alone on a windswept landscape. Take over, it's your turn. Pick a path. Why not? Kids are at stake. New leaders must come forward.

Processes to facilitate transformation may bring order to change program. A myriad of experiences can be designed to help a mature organization seek a new future in a new age. In fact, so many consultants are on the circuit, so many books hit the stands, and so many new techniques spill out from the pages of professional periodicals that appropriate selection and match may be difficult. One might end up with a floozy costume from the mix and match section of the Goodwill Store contrasted with a perfectly coordinated dress-for-success daywear.

Someone must be appointed to keep the total effect in mind. The change process is actually composed of stages in a developmental order. These development stages can guide a seeking faculty.

Awareness of national scene

Awareness of who you teach

Information to change your mind

Sense of movement afoot

Paradigm shift commitment

Willingness to be led

Taking barbs to align with the new

Taking initiative to adopt and adapt

Speaking for program

Becoming excited about the future you can create

It is interesting to note that these process stages reflect other research studies based on widely accepted developmental stage theories. One is the *cognitive dissonance model.* It suggests that change occurs when individuals have experiences that lead to detection of a difference in what they believe and have believed for many years and what new knowledge now has them know.

These change stages also can be overlaid with Bloom's (1956) taxonomy, or hierarchal stages of cognitive thought. Piaget (1969) fits also.

Now that the strategic direction is in mind, tactical plans are in order.

THE LAY OF THE LAND

Step one: **Describe the nature of the children served. Who are they?**

Preparation: Study the demographics of the school's students and community in both national and local arenas:
         poverty level
         minority status
         handicapped
         single family homes
         trends until the next century
         grade analysis
         discipline records
         personal interviews
         mobility rate
         achievement trends
         learning styles

Action: Conduct a series of faculty meetings to present the results.

Artifact: Census data for any attendance area can be ordered from the data center of a state university.

Step two: **Discern the character of the staff in terms of their personality traits and flexibility to create change.**

Preparation: Gather data through:
Meyers Briggs Type Indicator (1987)
Faculty learning styles
Hemisphericity
Bernice McCarthy (1987)

Action: Hold a retreat at which time the staff considers themselves personally and studies the staff composite profile that describes those who are the change initiators. Discuss the potential for change to occur. What will be weaknesses and what will be strengths?

Artifact: A sample learning style profile from Dunn and Dunn (1985)

Step three: **Create school structures that accommodate change.**

Preparation: Study the leadership configuration to determine if there are three types of groups—problem solving groups, long range planning groups, and communication groups.

Action: Initiate groups to perform those functions not currently performed or those performed inadequately. Ensure that each group has a clearly understood purpose and a designed method of operation including how it will be led, how it will make decisions, and how its meetings will be conducted.

Artifact: Create a graphic of leadership configuration

Step four: **Raise the level of knowledge**

Preparation: Survey staff's current knowledge in regard to instructional methodology, learning principles, new research, and state of the art thinking.

Action: Form a group to be responsible for raising the knowledge level and improving the practices of the faculty. Make a plan for one year of intensive workshop attendance including a structured way to share knowledge and observe practices through such techniques as peer coaching. These sessions could be an hour after school once a week for two months, two release days during a semester, paid overtime, or any other feasible method.

Artifact: Staff Needs Assessment (Figure 1)

Step five: **Reorient all school structures to support student success.**

Preparation: Identify structures in the school that tend to accommodate an acceptance of student failure:
> grading system
> homework policy
> attendance procedures
> tracking
> lack of resources for outplacement
> outmoded philosophies in such areas as
>> motivation and achievement
> role of counselors, administrators

Action: Use the appropriate leadership groups to eliminate rituals and customs that do not promote student success and formulate new rituals and customs that will promote student success. For example, some teachers may give up power tests that assume some level of student failure in favor of performance tests that allow for the possibility that all students may perform very well.

Figure 1

MIDDLE SCHOOL NEEDS ASSESSMENT

Please mark one X in the top section, and one X in the bottom section
for each numbered item

	1 Tracking	2 Objectives	3 Grouping	4 Mastery Learning	5 Learning Styles	6 Cooperative Team Learning
THEORY: A. I have not had an opportunity to learn this.						
B. I understand the theory, but not the details on how to use it.						
C. I have tried some techniques, but don't fully understand the theory.						
D. I feel very knowledgeable about this theory.						
PRACTICE: A. I have not tried this.						
B. I have tried some techniques, but am not thoroughly pleased with the results.						
C. I have tried some techniques and need to implement further.						
D. I use this concept regularly in class with good results.						

Artifact:	Time allocation wheel from Missouri Model Guidance Program (1986, 1993). This shows the recommended time allotments for counselors. The circle idea could be used to analyze current time usage of principals and teachers and contrast with desired allotments. (Figure 2)

Step six: **Direct the problem solving group to create a vision.**

Preparation:	Collect professional articles that point the way to a new vision.
Action:	Convene the long range planners to be trained in visioning. In weekly meetings, they can propose a written vision statement and engage the faculty in seeking consensus.
Artifact:	Sample vision statement. (Figure 3)

Step seven: **Formulate the school's core values**

Preparation:	Select a group to study the definition of core values. Prepare a set of statements that are examples of a goal, a mission, and a core value statement as models to differentiate among the types of statements.
Action	Convene the communicators to adopt those core values with the long range planners providing the mission statement.
Artifact:	Sample core values. (Figure 4)

Step eight: **Prepare a 5 year plan**

Preparation:	During the training for long range planners, this group suggests a plan to focus the school's improvement efforts.

Figure 2

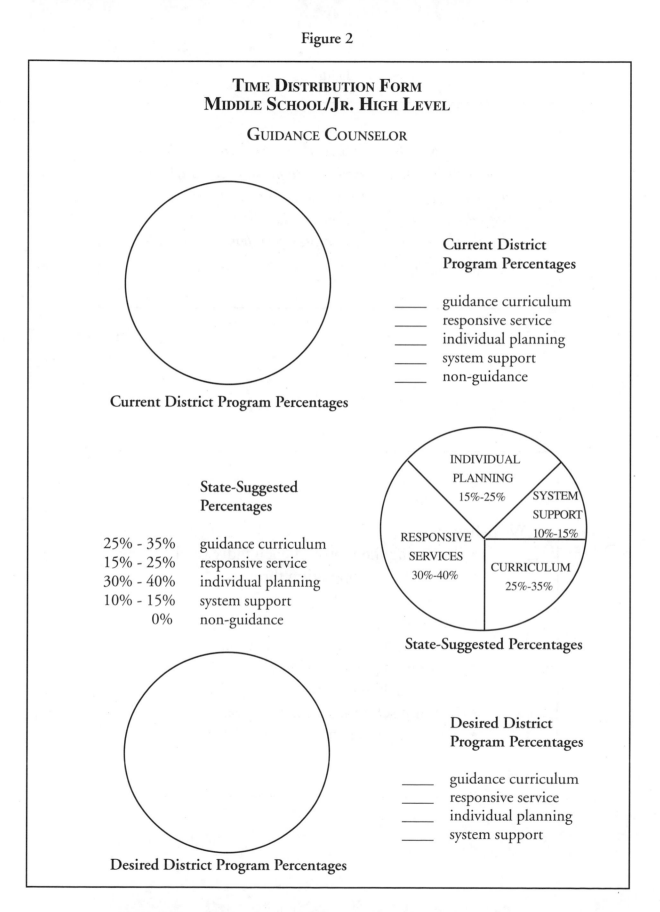

TIME DISTRIBUTION FORM
MIDDLE SCHOOL/JR. HIGH LEVEL

GUIDANCE COUNSELOR

Current District Program Percentages

Current District
Program Percentages

_____ guidance curriculum
_____ responsive service
_____ individual planning
_____ system support
_____ non-guidance

State-Suggested
Percentages

25% - 35%   guidance curriculum
15% - 25%   responsive service
30% - 40%   individual planning
10% - 15%   system support
0%   non-guidance

INDIVIDUAL
PLANNING
15%-25%

SYSTEM
SUPPORT
10%-15%

RESPONSIVE
SERVICES
30%-40%

CURRICULUM
25%-35%

State-Suggested Percentages

Desired District
Program Percentages

_____ guidance curriculum
_____ responsive service
_____ individual planning
_____ system support

Desired District Program Percentages

Figure 3

Cross Keys Middle School dedicates itself to the service of children. Its mission is to produce self-sufficient citizens who are adaptable to change and who possess the self-esteem, motivation, and skills to continue individual growth, solve complex problems, and respect cultural differences.

Figure 4

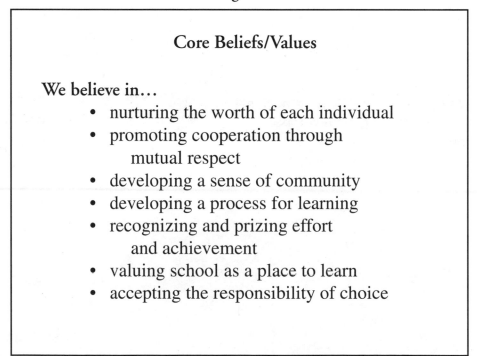

Core Beliefs/Values

We believe in...
- nurturing the worth of each individual
- promoting cooperation through
      mutual respect
- developing a sense of community
- developing a process for learning
- recognizing and prizing effort
      and achievement
- valuing school as a place to learn
- accepting the responsibility of choice

Action:	The planners present the plan to the problem solvers to be confirmed by the staff as a whole, making the vision one that has been suggested by the faculty.
Artifact:	Sample five year plans. (Figures 5 and 6)

Step nine: **Construct a yearly building plan that adds objectives and activities to the five-year plan.**

Preparation:	Identify time during team planning for teams to set annual improvement plans in support of the building improvement plan.
Action:	Each team should reveal its plan to others in a faculty meeting.
Artifact:	Sample building plan. (Figure 7)

Step ten: **Administrators should link teacher evaluation processes to the team and building plans.**

Preparation:	Analyze the teacher evaluation plan for suitability. The heart of improvement processes is for every individual in the organization to set personal goals systematically.
Action.	Hold individual conferences with every teacher in accordance with the agreed upon teacher evaluation plan to determine activities that teachers will pledge to complete during the year. Use scheduled observations and feedback sessions to elicit teacher's support of building improvement efforts.
Artifact:	Sample professional growth plan. (Figure 8)

Step eleven: **Seek rewards.**

Preparation:	Look for grants, district recognition, or other rewards.

Figure 5

CROSS KEYS FIVE YEAR PLAN
GROWTH INDEX

COMPONENTS	86-87 Year 01	87-88 Year 02	88-89 Year 03	89-90 Year 04	90-91 Year 05
RELATIONSHIP...	Parental	――	――	IN-SERVICE	ADVISOR
TEACHER ORGANIZATION...	Interdisciplinary Teams	Interdisciplinary Teams	Interdisciplinary Teams	DEVELOP-MENTAL TEAMS	――
CURRICULUM...	Skills via Drill: Content Emphasis / IN-SERVICE	SKILLS VIA DRILL: CONTENT APPLICATION / IN-SERVICE	Skills Via Application: Activity Orientation / IN-SERVICE	Application Activity	――
SCHEDULE...	Block	――	IN-SERVICE	DEVELOP-MENTAL	――
INSTRUCTION...	Teacher-Directed		Teacher-Directed Student-Directed	――	――
GROUPING...	Grade / IN-SERVICE	Grade	MULTI-GRADE	DEVELOP-MENTAL	――
BUILDING PLANS...	Classroom Areas by Team	――	――	――	Team Areas
EXTRA-CURRICULAR...	INTEREST	――	――	――	――

Shaded Areas=Year's Emphasis

Figure 6

→ *WORKING DRAFT*

CROSS KEYS FIVE YEAR PLAN

	90-91 01	91-92 02	92-93 03	93-94 04	94-95 05
CURRICULUM	IMPLEMENT GRANT	REFINE ACTIVE CURRICULUM	EVALUATE RESULTS		
SOCIAL SERVICES	IDENTIFY NEEDS	IDENTIFY RESOURCES	IMPLEMENT NEW SERVICES	EVALUATION OF SERVICES	
INSTRUCTION	IMPROVE SCHOOL COMMUNICATION	EXPAND EXPLORATION	MULTI-GRADE GROUPING	REFINE MULTI-GRADE GROUPING	
SCHOOL CULTURE	IMPROVED TEAM PROCESS	CELEBRATE SUCCESS	EXAMINE SCHOOL PROCEDURES	REDESIGN SYSTEMS	REDESIGN SYSTEMS

Statement of Need/Problems

Priority Ranking	Description of Need/Problem	Evidence of Need/Problem
	The faculty has implemented interdisciplinary teams block scheduling, and an exploratory program; however, an imbalance of interdisciplinary teaching exists among the teams.	Two of six teams have developed and implemented interdiscplinary units taught by all six teachers, while other teams have only two teachers cooperatively teaching a unit. Still others have developed and cooperatively taught only one or two activities.

Statement of Goals

Building Goal	School District Goal
To establish Cross Keys as a fully functioning middle school. • a staff knowledgeable about and committed to middle school education • an appropriate active curriculum • an individual advisement program	To establish the middle school as an independent entity in the district's K-12 program.

Action Plan

Objectives	Activities	Who is Responsible	Time Table	Evaluation Procedures	Budget
To meet the needs of Cross Keys students	• assess the special needs of students				
	- identify students with special needs through the use of the Special Needs Identifier	COUNSELORS			
	- initiate design of program(s) aimed at addressing student's special needs	PRINCIPALS			

Figure 8

INDIVIDUAL TEACHER PROFESSIONAL GROWTH PLAN

name deleted
_____
Teacher

1. **Criterion:** My overall goal is to develop and implement a cohesive curriculum plan for both the reading and writing portions of the Workshop class, coordinating and dovetailing the disparate "content" of the reading materials with various appropriate writing modes.

2. **Objectives:** To achieve this goal, the following objectives must be accomplished:

   1. explore and determine the various modes of writing that are appropriate for seventh grade student needs and interests both within the confines of my specific course and within the larger framework of overall seventh grade curricular demands.

   2. determine which central writing mode/model will serve as a focus for most assignments for each quarter of the school year.

   3. determine an instructional sequence of writing modes/models that is incrementally more challenging each quarter.

   4. develop lesson plans which teach the specified writing mode/model and provide a wide range of student choice of topic and approach within the confines of a specific mode/model.

   5. enhance transfer of writing skills by the development of formats or writing frames for student Lit Log entries which use the specified quarter's writing mode/model wherever appropriate.

   6. introduce students to the literary vocabulary which they will use in their book analyses and responses in their Lit Logs.

   7. determine a sequence for the study and application of literary vocabulary to student reading that is incrementally more challenging each quarter.

   8. explore adaptations of the Atwell Reading Workshop model that will facilitate individual literary study of student-chosen reading materials.

3. **Procedures for achieving objectives:**
   In order to demonstrate the achievement of these objectives, I will:
   1. devise a quarter by quarter "course" outline indicating writing mode focus, sequence of instruction (both writing and literary vocabulary), and sample instructional lessons, accompanied by a narrative rationale and/or evaluation.

   2. produce an "artifact" collection of student work reflecting different writing modes, literary analysis, and personal reactions.

   3. attend conferences to glean ideas for the improvement of writing instruction and adaptations of the Atwell model and incorporate/adapt those ideas for incorporation into my class where appropriate.

4. **Appraisal method and target dates:**
   I expect that the achievement of my objectives to be appraised largely through the examination of course outline document and the student work artifact collection by my supervisor at the end of the time period covered by this PGP. In addition, I would expect periodic informal check conferences would be held throughout the duration of Professional Growth Plan period between myself and my supervisor. The frequency, length, and the necessity of "annotation" of these conferences I would leave up to the discretion of my supervisor.
   In order to accomplish my overall goal, I think that a two-year time period is needed, especially since a formal outline of the Reading Workshop section of the course has been fairly nebulous up to this time AND the Writing Workshop component of the course is in its first year of incorporation in the school curriculum. Given these facts, a target date of May, 1993 seems appropriate.

Teacher signature _____   Date _____

Supervisor signature _____   Date _____

Action: Lead a team to seek recognition of the progress made to date.

Artifact: Sample school recognition invitation. (Figure 9)

Step twelve: **Identify barometers of success.**

Preparation: Study Stufflebeam's (1985) Content, Context, Process and Product Model of evaluation.

Action: Determine those data that will show transformational progress. Don't ignore stories.

Artifact: Graph of shift of stanines. (Figure 10)

Step thirteen: **Create a field of dreams**

Preparation: Identify six or seven of the best abstract thinkers in the school or in its support network. Invite them to participate in a creative endeavor of designing a curricular architecture. Make sure they understand that they must come to the group simply as good thinkers not representative of any particular segment of the school's stakeholders. Prepare for the meeting. Plan on the task taking three days. A comfortable site is important. An outside consultant from the area of school improvement who is accustomed to facilitating design teams might be helpful.

Action: Conduct a three day design team work session. The end product should be a design for a curriculum whose essential nature reflects the basic beliefs of the mission statement, the core values, the school vision, and the knowledge base.

When the design is created, care must be taken to see that the design encompasses all the changes the faculty intends. To articulate these changes, the design group may wish to complete a paradigm shift outline that targets what the prevailing conditions of the curriculum are at the time the improvement effort is

Figure 9

Please join us for the festivities
celebrating the presentation of
The 1989 Excellence in Education Award
to Cross Keys Middle School
by the U.S. Department of Education
Thursday, December 14 at 7 p.m.
Florissant Civic Center
Florissant, Missouri

Dr. M. Dolores Graham, Principal
Faculty and Students

Figure 10

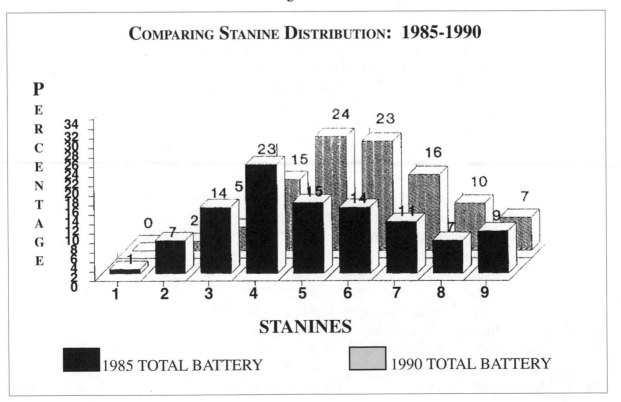

COMPARING STANINE DISTRIBUTION: 1985-1990

started, the condition to which the school intends to shift and what means will be used as curricular change elements.

On page 94 is a change matrix from the Metro 2000 Curricular Architecture that promoted Home Base Centers in the community. (Figure 11)

Holman School was attempting to transform itself through not only redesigning their curriculum architecture but also encompassing a broad-spectrum social services agenda. Their change matrix shows the congruence between design and proposed actions. (Figure 12)

At some point, the years the design team professionals have spent practicing their art and craft will take flight. Here is a journal entry from a principal who observed a design team at work:

> Come with me. I'd like to introduce you to the Graham Crackers' Team as they plan.
>
> The first thing we see is what appears to be confusion and disarray. Six teachers sit around a table littered with papers, donuts, and Doritos. On the wall are the beginnings of a mural. It appears to be symbolic of a cruise or voyage that the team make-believes they are going to take. This mythical trip serves as their personal motivator.
>
> As they begin to plan a new interdisciplinary unit, the mural is bare and the table is full of snacks. One teacher stands in front, fielding the ideas that the teachers suggest as themes or concepts they feel should be taught to their unique group of students. This group of teachers represents the type of students they teach, all uniquely different with a set of talents they wish to share with their students.
>
> It is impossible to distinguish the math teacher from the science teacher. They are focused on a theme, not on content. They are excited, noisy,

Figure 11

PARADIGM SHIFTS LEADING TO EDUCATIONAL CHANGE

FROM	TO
Emphasis on schooling.	The learner as the focus of all activity.
Students that are passive, rote learners.	Active discovering and reflective learners.
Students that are irresponsible, unethical, uncaring, and sometime violent.	Non-violent, caring, ethical, responsible citizens.
Textbook and teacher-dominated curriculum.	Curriculum that is authentic, active, and contextual.
Single classroom within four walls.	Off-site experiences—such as extensive use of the new St. Louis Science Center.
Disciplines isolated and organized around subjects and grade levels.	Interdisciplinary themes and multi-age divisions.
A place where professionals isolate themselves from the community.	A place where professionals work (and network) in the community as a whole.
A place where professional growth and development occurs in isolation.	A place where professionals see themselves as a community of learners and where continuous growth is an expectation.
A focus on measuring only verbal and quantative intelligence.	Accommodating a diversity of learning styles and multiple intelligences.
Paper/pencil, narrowly focused testing.	A broad range of assessment tools: performance based, portfolios, projects.
Parents as spectators of their children's learning.	Informed and engaged partners in their own and in their childrens' learning.
A limited access to and availability of technology.	The ability of technology to be applied by students, teachers, administrators, as they wish and need it.
Governance that is top-down.	Governance that is democratic and inclusive of all clients and employees.

Strategies to

help accomplish

our goals

Figure 12

HOLMAN'S CHANGE MATRIX		
FROM	TO	BY
Emphasis on schooling.	The learner as the focus of all activity.	Designing curriculum and instructional activities which have high transfer to the personal experiences of our children.
Textbook and teacher dominated curriculum	Curriculum that is authentic, active, and contextual.	Learning centers where children are active participants both in selecting appropriate activities and in the evaluation of their progress.
Single classroom with four walls.	"School Family" groups, skill groups, and age groups of student teacher ratios as follows: 7/1 "Family Groups" 15/1 Skill Groups 15/1 Multi-age Groups	Redesigning teacher student schedules and integrating support staff into the regular learning center process.
Sporadic, single event inservice on eclectic topics.	Sustained personal experience of great impact.	Providing a daily Instruction Fellow in the classroom to initiate a process for sustained growth after the grant period.
A place where professional growth and development occurs in isolation.	A place where professionals see themselves as a community of learners and where continuous growth is an expectation.	Immersion in cooperative efforts between staff and staff development fellows throughout the instruction process.
A focus on measuring only verbal and quantitative intelligence.	Accommodating a diversity of learning styles and multiple intelligences.	Matching children heterogeneously for learning style, cross age groupings and cross skill groupings to ensure all children will achieve a measure of success.
Paper/pencil, narrowly focused testing.	A broad range of assessment tools.	Observation data, gathering information through portfolios, child and parent centered assessment of the child's interest in school and skill levels.

and creative. As the members of the group share ideas and plans, the mural on the wall develops piece by piece. Like their students, they need positive reinforcement. Each time a new idea is contributed, the group adds another piece of the "cruise." The mural takes shape with a palm tree, a ship, and an island.

As they plan, they make sure that the preferred learning styles of their students are met. Sometime during this unit all of the students will be actively engaged, as they themselves are, in planning the unit. A variety of teaching strategies and materials will be used. By the end of the week, the mural is full and the table is bare.

Let's contrast this scene of a curriculum in transformation with a look at the operation of a more traditional team meeting.

Again, six teachers are seated around the table. They are planning the schedule for the upcoming weeks. One teacher says, "I need to have my students for three one hour time periods so that I can use the computer lab for a simulation activity." The others look at their own plan books to see if they can modify their plans to accommodate this request.

"I have a math test scheduled for Tuesday. If the kids don't have enough time to finish, will you see that they complete it?"

A deal is struck. They then work on modifying the students' schedules. Next, the team leader gives a report on a committee meeting she attended. The counselor then updates them on information about some of their students. The bell rings, and the meeting is over.

As we look at these examples of team meetings, we can see the growth that is evident. No longer is the focus mainly on the business of schooling (bell schedules, admission slips, school calendars). The team process has evolved and grown. This maturation has evolved over several years. The school went through a carefully planned process to encourage the growth of team interactions.

We developed a shared belief system which stems from a mission statement and a set of core beliefs.

Together Everyone Achieves More—TEAM

Much was shared on topics such as: the characteristics of effective middle schools, the nature of learning, and the concept of individual learning styles.

We validated the belief that accommodating individual learning styles is a way to assure that all students become actively engaged in their own learning. Students must be engaged in a manner that allows the teacher first to join the students in their own world and only then lead them into an adult world. The developmental needs of students are the foundations of all instruction and interdisciplinary teaming.

It has been stimulating and rewarding to watch the creativity not only of individuals, but also more importantly of teams as they matured. We have discovered that there is actually a continuum of growth in the teaming process. Each succeedingly higher level evidences greater integration and sophistication than the level below it.

Level 1: Teachers cooperate with each other, sharing students and time.

Level 2: Teachers share common resources such as materials, space, time, or funds.

Level 3: Teachers agree upon a shared skill that all subject area specialists will teach through their content areas. (A shared skill might be locating and working with the main idea in their social studies and science texts and then in the papers of their peers in their language arts class.)

Level 4: Teachers agree upon thematic units which can connect the students' learnings across disciplines. As they plan the subtopics and activities, each teacher selects those from their traditional content area curriculum that fit the theme.

Level 5: Teachers agree upon a concept which connects the students' learnings but has no content specialization and draw objectives and activities from their wide range of human talents and experiences both in and outside of their formal training and areas of certification. Once again, they become human beings competent and experienced in life itself, first, and in content areas only incidentally.

We realize that there are many definitions of teaming, but the teams we saw at work just must be parts of the door into creating a place of our own.

No one can describe creation. Even the Bible couldn't get much beyond saying that on the fifth day, He created the whales and all the winged fowl. (Genesis 1:21)

But the stage is set. "If you build it ..."

THE TEAPOT

I once saw an amazing teapot. Like a silver one. It had a floppy lid so that the liquid contents could leak out if one were not careful. The liquid is really supposed to come out of this long arching spout attached to the pot's side. It is one of those family heirlooms that no company seems good enough to use. (They tarnish, too.)

Now, this one I saw looked not quite right somehow. For there right below the spout was its handle. One side was completely bare, the other side was doubly blessed.

My, my, I thought, this teapot has the wrong idea. It is utterly useless. Even Alice In Wonderland could not pour and handle on the same side. I wondered if there is anything in my life that is so screwed-up?

And then, it struck me: I could not tell you why. But it struck me that there was some similarity between that pot and advisement programs. Could it be, I wondered, that people are designing advisement programs that are utterly use-less—because they are based on the wrong idea? People think advisement should occur only in groups when it really should occur only in one-to-one conferences —individually. Maybe advisement is not flowing well many places because of this fatal structural flaw.

No one knows why a silversmith with a warped sense of humor made such a contorted teapot, but we can figure out why advisement planners make their mistake. Schools only think of students in groups. We move them in groups.

We feed them in groups, and we teach them in groups. It is not surprising that, of course, advisement is scheduled in a group framework; yet if we agree that the purpose for advisement is to develop a relationship with each child, it makes perfect sense that advisement occurs best when an advisor and an advisee meet alone.

We can avoid a teapot caper. An advisement program can be totally individual. That means we can avoid food drives, candy sales, punching green tickets, forming circles, electing officers, raffling cold turkeys, and other things advisors are heir to.

What we do is find common ground with a student and have dialogues. Long talks. Short talks. Some paper. Some tasks. All activity is initiated simply to allow a forum for a relationship to develop, to flourish. Perhaps this natural logic: *if you want to build a relationship, go find the person and start one* is too straightforward. Surely it can't be that way, but it is so.

Chapter Eight

Taking an Individual Path

ebaters, jealous colleagues, distraught parents, over-zealous media and even a used-to-be best friend will become major detracting forces, all at some point in the transformation process. As the exciting change process unfolds, transformational leaders must prepare themselves to maintain equilibrium in the face of mighty challenges. Mental preparation can be a protective armour for the point/counterpoint score that is surely to come.

Point

But they won't be ready for high school.

Counterpoint

The best preparation for high school tomorrow is to actively engage youngers in learning today.

Point

What was good enough for me should be good enough for them.

Counterpoint

The playing field has changed. Don't restrict the children of the 90s to old solutions for a world that no longer exists. There is no research to support current practices.

Point

Our test scores will go down.

Counterpoint

Trust me. Norm referenced tests will continue to distribute students along the same normal curve distribution as students keep on learning without regard to specific content learned. Some early studies are now coming from transforming middle schools with encouraging data. The emerging picture is that norm referenced student achievement performance is positively affected by appropriate changes in middle school curriculum integration.

Point

Everybody can't get an "A".

Counterpoint

Why can't they? Good teaching and good curriculum produce success for students. Success for all is a very legitimate goal for schools.

Point

My kids are bright. Don't hold them back by putting them with all the other kids.

Counterpoint

America will not survive under such an elitist attitude and there is no research to support the practice of ability grouping.

Point

The school doesn't have any money.

Counterpoint

There are boot straps you know. Use them.

Point

How do we know we are going the right way?

Counterpoint

To excel is to risk more than others think is wise. Risk-taking is an essential part of transformation.

Point

But will they learn grammar?

Counterpoint

The purpose of education is to develop multiple neural pathways, not learn specific bits of knowledge—but they will learn how to express themselves correctly in the process of pursuing meaningful activities. Whole language approaches and Nancie

Atwell's (1987) reading-writing workshop approach are examples of strategies that develop multiple neural pathways. In both examples, students also learn English content.

Point

Why do you want to change?

Counterpoint

We now know much more about how people learn than we did twenty years ago. We must turn our schools into places that promote learning based on our best knowledge of how people learn—information not available when present practices were instigated.

Point

I don't have time for this.

Counterpoint

Study what you do. Eliminate those ritualistic trappings of schooling. Time to structure a place for learning will emerge.

_____

But even the most vigorous debates can end in inaction. Many schools never initiate such dialogue, make long-range plans, or even consider their place and time. In such a static culture, individuals still can make an impact by designing their own curriculum architecture to be implemented in their own classroom or perhaps within their own team if like-minded teammates can be persuaded. Following a format can help individuals make decisions about what they are to teach and what students are to learn.

This format, just as school-wide architecture, should be based on the very best knowledge of how students learn. From this knowledge base, teachers should prepare their own change matrix as those illustrated in Chapter Seven. A sample entry might be:

From paper-pencil tests to performance checks by designing activities where skill acquisition can be observed.

These types of transformations are well within the teacher's locus of control.

It need not always be a design team that creates a curriculum architecture. A teacher planning a course or a unit can design an architecture. At a university in an advanced degree curriculum course, the course architecture takes the form of an icon that expresses three values the professor holds. The icon expresses the concept that in the course 1) students from diverse situations experience a coming together and 2) at other times, their diversity is applauded and accommodated, while 3) there are times in the course progression when students shape the course to suit their own needs by making choices.

These examples of curriculum illustrate that architecture must be created, congruent with a school's mission and philosophy. Curriculum architecture is the basic frame, or building block, of a plan of access.

DEVELOPING CURRICULUM UNITS AND PROJECTS

Once the teacher's change agenda is clearly identified through the creation of a change matrix, then the teacher can leave the architecture design stage and begin a developmental phase in which the teacher's plans of access for students reaches definition.

Once past the change matrix format, there are many curriculum development formats available to a teacher. Some districts have a districtwide format that has been adopted. Regardless of which format an individual uses for a final curriculum development product, the teacher must make critical decisions in the following areas when creating a unit.

A. Type of project: Decide what is to be developed: a course, a unit, a series of activities.

B. What need is the project meant to meet? Decide what specific problems have occurred using typical methods.

C. Evidence of the need: Decide what objective data proves this project is needed.

D. Special instructional strategies: Decide what new strategies will be used to constitute an improvement over common practice.

E. Student population: Decide what segment of the student population can benefit most from this new plan, such as grade level, skill level, interest level, learning style.

F. Goals: Decide what global exit learner outcomes will be achieved.

G. Objectives: Decide what product, performance, or artifact will be evidence of learner achievement of the outcome.

H. Classroom management plan: Decide how the teacher will manage groupings to organize students for activity, such as in cooperative learning groups,

I. Evaluation of the curriculum: Decide how the teacher will judge the success of the new effort as contrasted to previous practice.

J. Concept: Decide upon a concept as the central focus of the unit that is developmentally appropriate for students.

K. Materials: Decide what student materials are needed.

L. Activities: Decide what are the most authentic student experiences that could be created, leading to engaging students in searching for meanings connected to the concept.

M. Order: Decide what order of activities will produce the best results.

N. Step-by-step directions: Decide on a timeline and each day's directions.

O. To do list: Decide what materials will have to be created. These decisions will result in an individual teacher creating new curriculum. It should be noted that the order of the decisions may change if the format to be used not only guides decisions during the creative process but also is written for someone else to read. One order is best to use; another is best for reading.

The only rational approach for the future is to work in a culture that is characterized by a continuous improvement process. At a school level where a curriculum architecture has been designed and at the teacher level where teachers understand curriculum, architecture should be created with the goal of success for all children.

A Place of Our Own

In Robert Frost's poem, "The Hired Man," home is described as ". . . a place where when you go there, they have to take you in." We have come to believe that school is home for many youngsters. For some it is solace; for some it is a buffer, and for some it is a social gathering place. But in schools, we have not always made them feel very welcome. We have "taken them in," but we have build the place to suit ourselves. We have set the rooms up so that we can stand in front. We have build long hallways and then proceeded to police them. Even the way we interact with children is predominantly control oriented. We select the books; we select the activities; we adjust the pacing, all devoid of student choice. Because school is a home for many students and we are, to some degree, their family, our students deserve *A Place Of Our Own*:

a place where
> students and teachers spend their most productive
> moments;

a place where
> the relationship between a teacher and a student
> has a quality of wonder, of magic;

a place where
> everyone purposefully seeks to be better . . . to
> have competence, compassion, and potential;

a place where
> the "I cans" speak so loudly that the "I can'ts"
> cannot be heard;

a place where
> students and teachers stand by each other and say,
> "We will not let each other fail;"

a place where
> students and teachers applaud each other's successes;

a place where
> we experience the joy, the zest of life.

While we would like to believe that all students in every school are nurtured and that time is available for discovery, in reality individual interests are often thwarted by limited choice, predetermined learning activities, and highly structured time periods. Students at the elementary level are expected to learn skills through drill and practice. High school students choose from specific content areas to meet graduation requirements with limited options.

Middle schoolers need both skill and content; however, more importantly, during a time when they are searching for personal meaning and identity, they need opportunities to actively explore their world with others. They need a fail-safe environment in which they can question, experiment, create, and make decisions; a place where they are valued just because they are who they are. And since society does not readily have such places, we have to create one, *A Place Of Our Own*. It seems as though all middle schools are hunting for a special place, searching for this identity in the educational spectrum.

BIBLIOGRAPHY

Atwell, Nancie. (1987). *In The Middle: Writing, Reading, and Learning with Adolescents.* Upper Montclair, NJ: Boynton/ Cook Publishers, Inc.

Beane, James A. (1993). *A Middle School Curriculum: From Rhetoric to Reality, 2nd Edition.* Columbus, OH: National Middle School Association.

Benton, M. (1991). *The Illustrated History, Superhero Comics.* Dallas, TX: Taylor Publishing Company.

Bloom, Benjamin. (1956). *Taxonomy of Educational Objectives: Handbook I; Cognitive Domain.* New York: McKay.

Caine, N. C., and G. Caine. (1991). *Making Connections, Teaching and the Human Brain.* Alexandria, VA: Association for Supervision and Curriculum Development.

Carnegie Council on Adolescent Development (1989). *Turning Points: Preparing American Youth for the 21st century.* New York: Carnegie Corporation.

Cross, Christopher T. (1990). *Issue In Education. Who Is the American Eighth Grader?* NELS: 88. National Education Longitudinal Study of 1988. Washington DC: Office of Educational Research and Improvement. US Department of Education. US Government Printing Office.

Dunn, Rita and K. Dunn. (1982, 1985). *Learning Styles Model.* Lawrence, KS: Price Systems, Inc.

Ferguson-Florissant School District, Cross Keys Middle School. Missouri Department of Elementary and Secondary Education Incentive Grant: Active Learning In The Middle School. (1991). *A Place Of Our Own.* Florissant, MO: Ferguson-Florissant School District.

Greenwood, John, Editor. (1991). *Milestones of Aviation*: New York: Crescent Books.

Goodlad, John. (1984). *A Place Called School*. New York: McGraw-Hill.

Kaybee Goodtimes Magazine. (1992). Volume 1, Number 2, November-December. Encino, CA: RM Marketing, Inc.

Kids Count in Missouri. (1993). Citizens for Missouri's Children. Annie Casey Foundation and The Missouri Department of Elementary and Secondary Education. Jefferson City, MO: Missouri Department of Elementary and Secondary Education.

Kozol, J. (1991). *Savage Inequalities: Children in America's Schools*. New York: Crown.

Marzano, Robert J. (1988). *Dimensions of Thinking: A Framework for Curriculum and Instruction*. Alexandria, VA: Association for Supervision and Curriculum Development.

McCarthy, B. (1980, 1987). *The 4 MAT System, Teaching to Learning Styles with Right/Left Mode Techniques*. Barrington, IL: EXCEL, Inc.

Myers, Isabel B. (1964, 1987). *Introduction to Type*. California: Consulting Psychologists Press.

Norman, Donald A. (1988). *The Psychology of Everyday Things*. New York: Basic Books, Inc.

Ornstein, R., and P. Ehrlich. (1989). *New World, New Mind: Moving Toward Conscious Evolution*. New York: Doubleday.

Ornstein, R., and R.F. Thompson. (1984). *The Amazing Brain*. Boston: Houghton-Mifflin.

Piaget, Jean. (1969). *The Child's Conception of the World.* Totowa, NJ: Littlefield Adams.

Polite, Mary M. (1992). *The Story of Cross Keys Middle School: Learning to Ask the Right Questions.* Project Report. The National Center for School Leadership: University of Illinois at Urbana-Champaign, College of Education.

Sizer, Ted. (1992). *Horace's School.* Boston: Houghton Mifflin.

Starr, M., and N. Gysbers. (1988, 1989). *Missouri Comprehensive Guidance - A Model for Program Development, Implementation and Evaluation.* Jefferson City, MO: Missouri Department of Elementary and Secondary Education.

Stufflebeam, D.L. (1985). *Systematic Evaluation: A Self-instructional Guide to Theory and Practice.* Boston: Kluwer-Nijhoff.

The Holy Bible, The King James Version. (1976). New York: The World Publishing Company.

Twain, Mark. (1962 ed.). *The Adventures of Huckleberry Finn.* New York: Scholastic Magazines, Inc.

U.S. Children and Their Families: Current Conditions and Recent Trends. (1989). Select Committee on Children, Youth, and Families. US House of Representatives. Washington, DC: US Government Printing Office.

Vitale, Barbara M. (1982). *Unicorns Are Real.* Rolling Hills Estates, CA: Jalmar.